Entanglements of Two: A Series of Duets

EDITED BY
KAREN CHRISTOPHER AND MARY PATERSON

Contents

Opening Gambit

KAREN CHRISTOPHER

This book is about duets. Not duos, as we discuss in these pages, but an *other* form that is produced when two people work together. This careful distinction in language is important because a duet is a third element that emerges from its constituent parts. A duet is a creation, both more real and less real than the elements that made it possible.

This book is anchored in the work of my performance company, Haranczak/Navarre Performance Projects; specifically, it is anchored in over a decade of my practice working in duets with other artists including Gerard Bell, Teresa Brayshaw, Tara Fatehi Irani, Sophie Grodin and Rajni Shah. Like those duets, this book began as an invitation from me – or a series of invitations – each designed to expand beyond a single point of view. One of those invitations was to Mary Paterson, to co-edit the publication. Other invitations were sent to other performers, other artists, other writers and other people working in disciplines that are less often connected with performance: linguistics, pedagogy, physics.

The aim of the publication is to reflect on these third elements – that which happens when a duet is formed – and, as part of that process, to generate new ones.

Because sequencing is everything and every sequence tells a story (the story of the sequence), we have arranged the contents with an introduction that is more like a thread stitching through the book than a pile of words at the beginning. The usual transition from not reading to reading a book is all upfront; in this book, we have distributed it throughout and reflected back on the texts in the conclusion.

As co-editors, we are thinking about transitions and how they operate and how we make it from one moment to the next, drawing each receding moment into the oncoming one – healing the gaps with a moment of lingering, holding on for adjustment, bracing for change. With our distributed introductory fragments, we are acknowledging the many transitions encountered between the different pieces of writing that appear here. A reader (you) can certainly drop in at any moment, or follow a single thread, or follow a number of threads simultaneously. Apparently, a sentence in English can only say one thing at a time. We will see about that.

Since 2010, Mary has responded to the work of Haranczak/Navarre Performance Projects by composing creative responses, in written form, to the experience of attending our live events. They stand as works of art in their own right. These pieces now form Mary's contribution to the introduction. My introductory fragments attempt to convey a set of preoccupations that led to the conception of this book project.

In this way, we have tried to assemble the essays that make up this book into a continuous whole, while leaving them intact as individual entities. We are attempting to weave them together into a fabric of differentiated strands.

Foreword

SEASON BUTLER

Part One: The Urchin and the Octopus

When I was 11 years old, I lived with my parents and sisters in an apartment a few blocks from the National Zoo in Washington, DC.[1] There was a constant exchange between the smog of broad streets congested with big cars that, in the early nineties, had not yet fallen entirely out of favour and the impossible green of Rock Creek Park. This exchange was nearly imperceptible but much easier to notice during the slowdown of The Hundreds. The Hundreds refers to 100 days of 100° heat and 100% humidity that sets in the summer.[2] Under these conditions, you have to go slow – so slow that you can almost see the exhaust exhale and the trees inhale; so still that the city is perfect. Under these conditions, I would walk to the zoo, a place with air-conditioned buildings but without store detectives and fresh air without audacious, catcalling would-be paedos.[3]

And if I was quick, I could meet Arthur[4] there for lunch.

Static hugged the afternoon: the overcast white sky, the buzz of big brown beetles, the songs of cockroach wings and the odd abortive cicada. Mosquitos bit welts into my straight brown legs on summer days and I scratched the welts to big round scars and I was almost a juvenile giraffe, all limbs and knobbly joints, legging my way through the city.

I entered the Invertebrate House as black spots started to appear on the hot pavement with the onset of the afternoon rainstorm. Inside was close and clammy but a few precious degrees cooler. It took a while for my eyes to adjust to the dim, but I knew my way by rote. I admired the cuttlefish first and proceeded to the 'touch pool' where

1. This is not true. When I was 11 years old, it took me a bus and a Metro ride, with a short walk on each side of the journey, to reach the zoo.

2. My use of the term implies that it is a regional institution, a common local saying. It is not. And the mention of the specific temperature and humidity is hyperbole but not too far from the truth. I am basically *trying to make fetch happen* here.

3. The would-be paedos at the zoo did not catcall, so I did not know they were there.

4. Not his real name.

I teased anemones that tried to grab my fingers and let urchins' spines explore my palms until the time came to feed Arthur.

Arthur, the giant octopus. He had eight legs and three hearts – facts I admired but did not envy. I took my place for the feeding demonstration, watching him and pretending he was watching me. That day, his craggy skin was deep brown. I turned my arm and squeezed the skin of my elbow to compare.

Normally, the zookeeper would stake a shrimp through a long metal stick and walk it along the floor of the tank, letting Arthur hunt it as if in the wild.[5] I made small talk with the keeper, who recognized me from my frequent visits. She eyed me up with scrutiny, raised her eyebrows in a *come on, cheer-up, it can't be that bad* expression. I smiled back weakly, whereupon she asked whether, as I knew the drill, I would like to feed Arthur that day. My single heart leaped and my face formed the sincere smile people prefer from girls.

I climbed a step ladder to the top of the tank while the zookeeper narrated for the assembled tourists and day trippers. I staked the shrimp on the sharp end of the stick and plunged my arm in.

Arthur watched and strategized.

But when he finally did strike, it was to shoot a tentacle from under his coiled body, not to grab the dead grey shrimp, but the more substantial meat of my right arm. It spiralled up from my wrist to my shoulder with the speed and strength of absolute intent. There was a short splash as he pulled, and my chest hit the surface of the water. Arthur's grip was both elastic and unyielding, strange smooches from the animal I most admired, the outset of the contact so quick and wet, I was breathless and never wanted it to end. At some point, we made eye contact, and somehow, I knew that the event – what I would later decide was my life's very first *event* – would last as long as our eye contact. Indeed, my rescue came far too soon; the zookeeper rushed to my side, climbing the ladder next to me, then reaching into the water to soothe Arthur by rubbing his big, wrinkly mantle. After a long moment, he relaxed his grip; his colour changing from brown to the deep red of an anatomical heart. I withdrew my dotted arm and hoped the blush red suction-cup circles would leave scars.

5. The rest of this story is appropriated from the zookeeper's anecdote. Since I heard it, I tried it on as a lie so many times that it has become a memory. The story from here on is the lie I eventually gave up telling since no one ever believed it. But the memory of the lie is the best duet I have ever had.

This book is about performance-making processes in a specific unit of human togetherness (the duet) and creations orientated towards a larger and less discreet unit of human togetherness (the audience).

Consider the twosome. A cultural privileging of this configuration hovers. Elizabeth von Armim's narrator in *The Enchanted April* even suggests that people can 'only really be happy in pairs [...]'.

We meet one-to-one to have focus, a kind of shared privacy, in a group that is not big enough for us to use the word 'group'. The idea urges notions of intimacy, a word that comes up a lot in the meditations that follow. Twosomes give space for ideas to unfold *between you and me*. Just between you and me, keeping confidence of a kind. And yet, the outward orientation complicates the notion of secretiveness that might be implied here. Complication, tension, imbalance, selfishness: these are not just obstacles within the work-of-two, but central to its potential.

The twosome cuts both ways. The potential for balance and the echo of the symmetry we so often find in nature and culture (e.g. monogamous couples, paired limbs, creepy doppelgängers) is tempered by the vulnerability inherent in being alone together. Within this state of intimacy, we feel the pain of being misunderstood, ignored and overruled most acutely. Imbalances are heightened, and they are lonely in a pair. Break-ups are considered 'failures'. Impasses often require another party to resolve.

Spectators view twosomes from the outside. The audience of a duet sees the part of what happened between a you-and-me that the twosome choose to bring to the public sphere. But the processes themselves still have a presence in the finished product. This book affords us a view of processes that can (must?) accommodate ambiguity and ambivalence and which require a particular mode of sustained attention, negotiation and cooperation.

Most of you will read this book quietly, on your own, and enter into a kind of intimacy with what lies behind the performance work by teams and communities and families and gangs of two. *Between you and me*. Keep me company.

Haranczak/Navarre Performance Projects
Duet Collaborations, 2010–21

So Below
Collaborators: Gerard Bell and Karen Christopher
Performances: 2010–17

Control Signal
Collaborators: Karen Christopher and Sophie Grodin
Performances: 2012–17

Seven Falls, outdoor performance
Collaborators: Teresa Brayshaw and Karen Christopher
Performances: 2012–17

miles & miles
Collaborators: Karen Christopher and Sophie Grodin
Performances: 2015–17

Always Already
Collaborators: Karen Christopher and Tara Fatehi Irani
Performances: from 2021

The duet series is titled *The Difference Between Home and Poem*. Karen's company, Haranczak/Navarre, is named after the maiden names of her two grandmothers.

TwoFold, a festival of duet performances, took place at Chisenhale Dance Space (London, 2017), which included the following:
• three studio performances – *So Below, Control Signal* and *miles & miles* – presented in double bills alongside duet projects by other artists: Joe Kelleher and Eirini Kartsaki, R. Justin Hunt and Johanna Linsley, and Dan Watson with Matthew Winston;
• the outdoor performance, *Seven Falls*;
• two programmes of performance lectures, including Karen's collaborations with Lucy Cash, Chris Goode and Rajni Shah;
• public workshops and
• a related symposium on duet practices at Birkbeck Centre for Contemporary Theatre, London.

More information: http://karenchristopher.co.uk/

Introductory Fragment 1: The Two of You

KAREN CHRISTOPHER

Think of someone you know well and have a deep fondness for, someone whose company you enjoy. Imagine spending time with this person in a workroom where you will make something with them, something from nothing. It will take at least a month of days, possibly with some time apart in between work days, but when you are working, it is just the two of you.

Take a moment, you and I have time. Let us say we have no anxiety about the passage of time. What do you imagine happens there in that room? How do the two of you proceed? With this person you might do anything, focus on any thoughts, compose words and actions, make plans. But what actually happens? And how does it come about? I heard theoretical physicist Carlo Rovelli say particles that make up the world are not things, they are happenings. And he said, a stone is just something that has happened for a long time.[1] We are not happening as much or as long as a stone, but the fact that we experience time emotionally means this time we spend in the studio might not go as we imagine it right here right now in the context of this page or in the way it happens in our mental landscape.

I am always me because I am not you. But I am also aware that parts of me do not understand other parts of me, and this is true not just for me. Parts of us are conscious and parts of us are unconscious. The unconscious writes the book, the unconscious makes the performance, the conscious worries uncontrollably and declares disaster. It is too long, it is too short, it is too obvious, it is opaque. No one will understand you because we are all from separate races – each individual their own race with their own traditions and ceremonies. The anthropologists have been furloughed.

1. Carlo Rovelli at the Hay Festival, 27 May 2020, live online discussion, https://www.hayfestival.com/p-16801-carlo-rovelli.aspx. Accessed 22 December 2020.

Writing is somewhat similar to untangling a length of rope. Thoughts exist in simultaneity and a curvature of relations within my thoughtscape. In order to write them down and give a rational order to them, I attempt to put them in a grammatical line. I struggle to do this if I do not maintain some level of calm even through an emotional response. In that way, writing might demand calm from a troubled state of mind; it might settle a tangle of emotions; it might set into reason a confusion of if/then loops.

Consider the knot: the one that keeps the mast steady in heavy wind; the one that closes the umbilical cord; that joins two ropes together at a right angle; that, multiplied by many, comprises a bridge; that keeps a kite from flying away; that holds a ship at the dock; maintains a position at sea; measures the speed; frees a parachute from its package.

A rope is a finite thing, and you will get to the end of it. It is a solvable problem, the tangle of it. The untangling of it will take the time it takes; the quality of the rope is not something to bargain with. The tangle can be rectified given the time and patience to do it. It is either untangled or dissolved into its constituent parts. It holds together by the twist of two contradictory forces. Without those, it is just fibres reduced to gossamer, easily lost to the wind. Rope is unity, it is holding, it is stability, it binds together, it imprisons, it holds fast. It is right in front of us and fully comprehensible.

The entanglement created alone together with one other person is far less fathomable than any rope can muster.

Between Two Somethings

J. R. CARPENTER

A duet is the action produced by two of something. The action resides in neither one nor the other of the something. It is never either, always both. This chapter is concerned with the space between these two somethings. I use the word 'space' loosely. What *is* this between space? A place, a time, a page, an ocean. A mediatic relation. An awkward interloper. Between [what]? What is a variable here: between [space, time, us]. My interest is in the nature of between itself and its varieties of disturbance. This chapter considers 'between' as a third time/space – the duet's third wheel: a texture, an event, a palpable unfolding fraught with interruption, interpolation, intersection, static, loss, fracture and glitch.

Coming to terms

Let us say, for argument's sake, that I am one of these two somethings. When I say 'I', I do not always mean me. Sometimes, my 'I' is haunted by an absence. And, therefore, evokes a presence. A ghost, a past, a gap, a *lapsus*. I am a migrant. A double emigrant born of immigrants born of emigrants. I was born in Nova Scotia. New Scotland. The New World. In those parts, in those days, they used to say, 'you're not from here until you have a grandfather buried here'. So even where I come from, I come from away. This is the first duet: the dance between insider and outsider, self and other, home and away.

Sometimes, my 'I' is fictional. A figment of geography. I was born near Port Royal, site of the oldest permanent European settlement in North America, north of St. Augustine, Florida. Port Royal was established by Samuel de Champlain in 1605 in a region already known to the French as Acadie. In the 1520s, the Verrazano brothers – Italians sailing for France – named the region north of Chesapeake Bay after the classical Greek Arcadia. As the name migrated northeast in subsequent maps of the coast, the 'r' was lost in transcription. Arcadia became Acadia. In 1755, the English expelled the French from Acadia to Louisiana. From Acadian to Cajun, a misplaced place name became the name of the displaced people and travelled with them. In *Homelands and Empires*, Jeffers Lennox asserts, 'To talk about Acadia or Nova Scotia in the eighteenth century is to engage in an act of imagination. Empires were geographic fictions and the colonies [...] were little more than a collection of [...] Weak forts, hastily constructed trading posts, and small villages [...] in a land that was thoroughly controlled by Indigenous peoples' (2017: 3). The New World was founded in the national territory of Mi'kma'ki, which had already been inhabited by the native Mi'kmaq for at least 13,000 years. I was born in Mi'kma'ki. I am a settler. This is the second duet: the slippage between place and displacement, nation and territory, name and inscription.

Sometimes, I wish to refer to a subject position bordering on the plural, which is not quite we. For nineteen years, I lived in English-as-a-minority-language in Mohawk territory on the French-speaking island of Montreal. A tongue not my mother's rivers in my mouth. In 2009, I emigrated to the island of Great Britain. In England, my English will forever mark me as a foreigner. I am a dual citizen now, a double subject of the same Queen. Hyphenated, a fragmentary creature. I wish to use the dubious privilege of my white but not-quite English English to speak. Not for but from amongst. To find intersections. To articulate complex subject positions. To call attention. To want but not need a response. The 'never either, always both' nature of the duet allows for lopsided, awkward conversations. We could also call these dialectics. Or dialogics. Much of the way I'm working right now involves dialogue. Because speaking about the unspeakable *with someone* comes as a relief.

Sometimes, my 'I' is usurped. Over the past twenty years, I have mixed my own writing, drawing, programming and photography with images, texts, diagrams and maps cut and copied from old magazines and textbooks and source code 'borrowed' from dusty corners of the web. That last sentence, for example, was borrowed from another chapter, from another book (Carpenter 2019: 243). Do I have to use quotation marks if I am quoting myself, in conversation with myself? Medieval Romans built blocks of flats in the ruins of ancient Roman amphitheatres. Early-modern English poets pillaged the Latin satirists to flatter their patrons. Shakespeare was a known plagiarist, incorporating contemporary and classical sources alike. The Letterists and Situationists praised Lautréamont's praise of plagiarism as necessary to progress in order to advocate for creative destruction through détournement. Building on their work, in *The Beach Beneath the Street*, halfway through a chapter on plagiarism, McKenzie Wark states, 'Needless to say, the best lines in this chapter are plagiarized' (2011: 41), brilliantly laying bare the process of writing as it is unfolding. Can I/we be both of the two somethings? Past and present self, spoken and written self, copied and pasted self. This is a duet between reading and writing, quotation and appropriation, text and context.

When I say 'text', sometimes, I mean image. Since 1995, I have been using the internet as a medium to combine image and text into new and, hitherto impossible, nonlinear, multimedia, intertextual contexts. Maps have figured prominently in my web-based work, performing a form of duet that Walter Benjamin terms as a 'dialectical image' (Richter 2007: 61). Maps wilfully confuse distance and proximity, image and interface, place and placeholder. My early adoption of the internet as a medium was due in part to my attraction to the web as an in-between space wherein the duets of image and text and map and trace may finally unfold. Many of my web-based works may be read as duets between longing and belonging. Websites becoming placeholders for pasts that could never be mine.

Writing coastlines

Other times, when I say 'text', I refer to physical terrains scored with human and non-human inscriptions. Let us say, for argument's sake, that the space between the two somethings is ocean. The first part of the title of my PhD thesis, *Writing Coastlines* (Carpenter 2015), implies a double meaning. It refers to writing *about* coastlines. It also suggests that the coastlines themselves are actively engaged in acts of mark making. Coastlines are edges, ledges and legible lines caught in a double bind between writing and erasing. These lines can be unstable, treacherous even, pitted with obstacles – crumbling cliffs, sea frets, wrecked ships, rip tides and all manner of hidden rocks, sand bars, shallows and shoals. And they can be porous, riddled with known ports as well as hidden coves, points of arrival as well as departure, carrying with them associations of refuge as well as of escape.

Coastlines constitute what Alexander Galloway terms 'interfaces': 'thresholds [...] mysterious zones of interaction that mediate between different realities [...] autonomous zones of activity [...] processes that effect a result' (2012: vii). For Galloway, interfaces both 'bring about transformations in material states' (vii) and, at the same time, 'are themselves the effects of other things, and thus tell the story of the larger forces that engender them' (vii). Not only does the cliff cause the wave to crash and the wave cause the cliff to crumble but also the wave may be high because of the tide and the cliff may be soft because of heavy rain, and the tide may be high and the rain may be heavy because of the larger force of climate change brought about by increased carbon emissions brought about by increased industrialization brought about by a complex combination of social and technological factors. A coastline, singular. Impossible. A linguistic foible. A coastline is never a solo act. It is always a duet, performed at the threshold between land and sea, solid and liquid, dry and wet.

One coastline implies another, implores a far shore. The spatiality and temporality of this entreaty intrigue me. When does leaving end and arriving begin? When does the emigrant become the immigrant? What happens between call and response? In *Writing and Difference*, Jacques Derrida asks, 'Is not the writing of the question, by its decision, by its resolution, the beginning of repose and response?' (1978: 76). The act of locating a distant shore provides a context for the fact of our present position, which is always already in the past, already behind us. In her long poem, 'The Fall of Rome: A Traveller's Guide', Anne Carson writes,

> A journey [...]
> begins with a voice
>
> calling your name out
> behind you.
> This seems a convenient arrangement.
>
> How else would you know it's time to go? (1995: 75)

This is another duet: between the past and the not quite yet.

Castaway questions

In castaway literature, the condition of being between places produces unanswerable questions. There being no one to answer and no one to answer to, the questioner is relegated to a realm outside the recursive. In 'A Topical Paradise', Hernán Díaz observes, 'the maroon embodies the contradiction of being a speaker without a society [...] Island narratives are, to a large extent, the account of desperate attempts at inventing an interlocutor' (2010: 83). Daniel Defoe's archetypal castaway *Robinson Crusoe* lists among the evils of his condition: 'I have no soul to speak to, or relieve me' ([1719] 2000: 50). His parrot Poll pesters him with questions:

> in such bemoaning language I had used to talk to him, and teach him, and he had learned it so perfectly, that he would sit upon my finger, and lay his bill close to my face, and cry, 'Robin, Robin, Robin Crusoe, poor Robin Crusoe! Where are you, Robin Crusoe? Where are you? Where have you been?' (109)

In Elizabeth Bishop's poem, 'Crusoe in England', the far shore implored by Crusoe shifts: from the shores of England as evoked when Crusoe is in exile to shores of the island of his exile when he returned to England. There is no repose for the questions Bishop's Crusoe poses. 'Do I deserve this?' (1984: 163). 'Why didn't I know enough of something?' (164).

Plagued her whole life by indecision, Bishop's – often parenthetically inserted – questions perform more like preponderances. In *Deleuze and Language*, Jean-Jacques Lecercle argues,

> A question is a temporarily suspended statement, the bloodless or ghostly double of the proposition it calls as its answer, whereas a problem, the site of creative thought, of the creation of thought, is never prepositional (it is formulated as a concept). (2002: 38)

A question and its answer: two somethings, but not necessarily a duet. Because, what is at stake? On one hand, an unanswerable question, and on the other hand, a waltz with loss. Loss is a problem. Gerhard Richter observes that an abiding sense of loss can then become 'the site on which dialectical thought unfolds' (2007: 36). What if we ask 'not what is the action produced by two of something, but where?' Not what is the problem, but where? Location, location, location. In her writings and in her life, Bishop returned again and again to coastal sites to explore in minute detail – through a combination of watching, walking, reading and writing – the problem of being in between places.

In 'Crusoe in England', the textual topography of the island poses a generative problem. Although it narrates a singular island in a single voice, we cannot say that this is a solo poem. Bishop's Crusoe's island bears no resemblance to Defoe's fictional island. *Robinson Crusoe* is loosely based on the Scottish sailor Alexander Selkirk's first-hand account of the Juan Fernández Islands, 670 kilometres off the coast of Chile, where he was marooned from September 1704 to February 1709. But Bishop's island does not resemble the Juan Fernández Islands either. Rather, it makes repeated textual references to Charles Darwin's descriptions of the Galapagos Islands as found in *The Voyage of the Beagle* ([1838] 1997), a book that Bishop 'admired, consulted, and drew upon' throughout her life (Doreski 1993: xiii).

Of the volcanically formed Galapagos, Darwin writes, 'One night I slept on shore on a part of the island where black truncated cones were extraordinarily numerous: from one small eminence I counted sixty of them, all surmounted by craters more or less perfect' ([1838] 1997: 356). In 'Caruso in England', Bishop wearily replies,

Well, I had fifty-two
miserable, small volcanoes I could climb
with a few slithery strides—
volcanoes dead as ash heaps.
I used to sit on the edge of the highest one
and count the others standing up,
naked and leaden, with their heads blown off. (1984: 162)

On one island of the Galapagos, Darwin admits, 'Although I diligently tried to collect as many plants as possible, I succeeded in getting very few' ([1838] 1997: 356). He later concedes that he mixed up collections from two separate islands: 'I never dreamed that islands, about fifty or sixty miles apart [...] formed of precisely the same rocks, placed under a quite similar climate, rising to a nearly equal height, would have been differently tenanted [...]' (374). In counterpoint, Bishop's Crusoe has nightmares of other islands:

[...] infinities
of islands, islands spawning islands,
like frog's eggs turning into polliwogs
of islands, knowing that I had to live
on each and everyone, eventually,
for ages, registering their flora,
their fauna,
their geography. (1984: 165)

Bishop's Crusoe's nightmares of other islands come partially true with his rescue to the island of Great Britain, which 'doesn't seem like one, but who decides?' (166). This thought is echoed by Susan Barton, the castaway narrator of another book in dialogue with *Robinson Crusoe*, J. M. Coetzee's novel *Foe*: 'They say Britain is an island too, a great island. But that is a mere geographer's notion. The earth under our feet is firm in Britain, as it never was on Cruso's island' ([1986] 2010: 26). Similarly, in 'A Topical Paradise', Hernán Díaz argues, 'One could even claim that Britain and Manhattan are not islands: despite being surrounded by water, they are far from being isolated, and each in its own way has extended beyond its shores' (2010: 79). In *Desert Islands*, Giles Deleuze argues that Britain and Manhattan are continental islands: 'Continental islands are accidental, derived islands. They are separated from a continent, born of disarticulation, erosion, fracture; they survive the absorption of what once contained them' (2004: 9). In J. G. Ballard's novel *Concrete Island*, the traffic island upon which the narrator Maitland becomes stranded is doubly continental: born of disarticulation from the urban mainland of London and derived from the literary mainland of Robinson Crusoe. Just as Crusoe is haunted by his own words spoken to himself repeated back to him by his parrot Poll, so too Maitland's words spoken to himself are haunted by the spectre of Crusoe: 'Maitland, poor man, you're marooned here like Crusoe – If you don't look out you'll be beached here forever [...]' ([1973] 2007: 32). In this archipelago of literary examples of dislocated duets, the castaway longs for an interlocutor precisely in order to articulate the impossibility thereof. There are not two of something but there *should* be.

Digital duets

My own process of reading across a corpus of castaway literature led to the creation of a web-based work called '...and by islands I mean paragraphs' (Carpenter 2013). My conflation of the terms 'island' and 'paragraph' in this title is informed by Díaz's suggestion that texts about islands are themselves islands:

> These textual shores (or *paragraphs*) are marginal in the triple sense that they are not part of the central body of text, that they are a physical space on the page that separates the text from the writer's desk or the reader's fingers, and that they surround and enclose the text in the same way that a margin surrounds or encloses a lake. (Díaz 2010: 83, emphasis added)

The space between the island and the mainland. The space between the castaway and the longed-for interlocutor. The space between the paragraph and the edge of the page. These are species of physical spaces that have been transformed by literature into commonplaces. With the advent of the digital literature, new conceptual reading spaces emerge. The space between the book and the web. The space between the web server and the reader's screen. The space between the hard drive and the skull's dark interior.

The in-between state has been articulated in terms of 'medium' in Western philosophy since classical times. In 350 BCE, Aristotle's articulation of air and water as 'betweens' transformed the Greek preposition 'between' into a philosophical concept: 'the medium'. Friedrich A. Kittler critiques Aristotle for not dealing 'with relations between things in time and space' (2009: 23–24) but, rather, relegating the concept of mediation to the realm of human sensorial perception. Kittler complains, '"In the middle" of absence and presence, farness and nearness, being and soul, there exists no nothing any more, but a mediatic relation' (26). Galloway dismisses Kittler's ontological critique of Aristotle as 'media-centric', 'reckless', 'foolishness' and 'rather vulgar' (2012: 15), advocating instead for a graduation in thinking, away from the device and 'into the deep history of media as modes of mediation' (15). This pragmatic approach frames the computer not as an object but rather as 'a process or active threshold mediating between two states' (23). Now, we are getting somewhere.

Like coastlines, digital texts can never be singular. N. Katherine Hayles argues that, in digital media, the text

> ceases to exist as a self-contained object and instead becomes a process, an event brought into existence when the program runs [...] The [text] is 'eventilized', made more an event and less a discrete, self-contained object with clear boundaries in space and time. (2006: 181–82)

Born of Cartesian binaries, of os and 1s and <head> <body> splits, digital texts continuously overflow the duet's formal boundaries. Too often, print and digital are set up as oppositional. Print is not a question for the digital to answer. New media of reading and writing do not constitute a rupture with the past. The 'never either, always both' nature of the duet is to consider the space between print and digital literature as intersectional, a site of exchange, an entanglement.

'...and by islands I mean paragraphs' casts a reader adrift in a sea of white space veined blue by lines of longitude, of latitude, of graph, of paper. The horizon extends far beyond the bounds of the browser window, to the north, south, east and west. Navigating this space (with track pad, touch screen, mouse or arrow keys) reveals that this sea is dotted with islands, and by islands, I mean small paragraphs of variable text. These fluid compositions reconfigure print texts in a digital literary context, inviting new readings.

One of the textual islands combines fragments from Bishop's poem 'Crusoe in England' and Darwin's descriptions of the Galapagos in *The Voyage of the Beagle*. In the source code, the island looks like this:

My island #{island} #{volcano}. #{climate} #{beaches}. As I walked along, #{walk}. The tortoises #{tortoises}. #{dreams}. #{complaint}

The variables {as indicated by curly brackets}, call on arrays (or lists) containing fragments from both texts. The computer selects fragments from these lists at random, regardless of authorship, to create an overtly intertextual island/paragraph. Here is an example of, but one of, a near infinite number of possible outputs:

My island seemed to have been permeated, like a sieve, by subterranean vapours. Immense deluges of black naked lava spread over miles of sea-coast. All the hemisphere's left-over clouds arrived and hung above the craters. The sun set in the sea; the same odd sun rose from the sea, and there was one of it and one of me. As I walked along, a large tortoise gave a deep hiss and drew in its head. The tortoises made excellent soup. I had nightmares of islands spawning islands, like frog's eggs turning into polliwogs of islands. Just when I thought I couldn't stand it another minute longer, Friday came. (Carpenter 2013)

Did I write this text? Is it a duet? If so, between whom? Crusoe + his island? Bishop + Darwin? Me + (Bishop + Darwin)? The Galapagos + England? JavaScript + the web browser? The web browser + this page?

I have quoted this text – signed my name to it, as if it actually exists. It did appear on a screen once, it must have done. Long enough for me to copy and paste it here. Where is here even? My computer + your page. But then, the computer made a new selection, because that's what I told it to do: play(45,000); a text spawning texts, like frog's eggs turning into polliwogs of texts. The chances of the computer ever generating this exact same text again are exceedingly slim. Perhaps this text is documentation then (of a duet [or a sequence of duets (a set of nested duets [asynchronous dialogues (snapshots of an ongoing digital process operating at the threshold between reading and writing)])])).

Thus far, I have focused on reading in an authorial sense, as part of writing. But what of the voice? Where does the body fit in? How can I, as a single body/voice, read/perform a digital text that is in fact many texts? Although it appears on screen as a single web page, '…and by islands I mean paragraphs' is actually an assemblage of 44 discrete .html, .js. and .gif files and a multi-authored jquery library. What is the point of reading aloud a text that has already been performed by a myriad of web server softwares and network protocols before reaching the screen? And even then. A shifty text, bound to change again every 45,000 milliseconds. A consistently unreliable collaborator. We can only conclude that the text on screen is a red herring.

The duet between my body and this unwieldy text takes place in a space between human and machine time, between human and machine reading. I cannot read as fast as the computer can. It cannot remember what it has written. I can. I can slow down the machine time by copying and pasting. The computer can only produce one text on screen at a time. But I can 'view source' to see the whole text, the subtexts that the computer has been ordered to keep hidden. And so, the performance script for our duet is necessarily written in neither JavaScript nor English but rather a bit of both. JavaScript is a procedural language. Like a script for live performance, JavaScript must be written and read in a particular order in order to be performed by the web browser. The JavaScript that generates the textual island (I mean paragraph) composed of fragments from Bishop and Darwin forces me to read both texts differently. I need to retain some of the syntax and grammar of the JavaScript to perform this new reading – and by reading, I mean talking.

The talk is an intermediary form between spoken and written text. To talk is to exchange ideas or relate narrative by speaking. A talk is an informal speech or lecture. A talk may be delivered from a written text, but it is a text written to be spoken. I created a print performance script to act as an intermediary between the fragments appropriated from print texts, the grammatical cues offered by the JavaScript syntax and my own spoken voice. This script was published under the title 'Ten Short Talks about Islands ...and by islands I mean paragraphs' in my debut poetry collection, *An Ocean of Static* (Carpenter 2018).

I close this chapter with the ninth talk/island/paragraph, in which, fragments from Bishop and Darwin are intermingled. Between you and me, I do not know who is who any more. There are a lot of us. We are a problem. We have found our middle ground on the page.

IX. Crusoe in the Galapagos.

My island ['- my brain bred island', '- a little world within itself', 'rose with a tame and rounded outline', '- caught on the horizon like a fly', 'smelled of goat and guano', 'seemed to be a sort of cloud-dump', 'seemed to have been permeated, like a sieve, by subterranean vapours', '- free to a remarkable degree from gales of wind']. My island had one kind of everything: ['one tree snail crept over everything', 'one variety of tree, a sooty, scrub affair', 'one kind of berry, a dark red', 'the goats were white, so were the gulls', 'when all the gulls flew up at once, they sounded like a big tree in a strong wind', 'the whole northern part miserably sterile', 'the whole lower region covered by nearly leafless bushes', 'such wretched-looking little weeds', 'the rocks on the coast abounded with great black lizards', 'a mouse, a rat distinct from the common kind', 'a most singular group of finches', 'one small lizard', 'one snake, which was numerous', 'thousands of huge tortoises', 'of toads and frogs there are none']. ['The hissing, ambulating turtles got on my nerves', 'I did not see one beautiful flower', 'Even the bushes smelt unpleasantly', 'I often gave way to self-pity.', 'Do I deserve this? 'Was there a moment when I actually chose this?', 'I didn't know enough.', 'Why didn't I know enough of something?', 'The books I'd read were full of blanks', 'Although I diligently tried to collect as many plants as possible, I succeeded in getting very few', 'I did not pay sufficient attention', 'None of the books has ever got it right']. (Carpenter 2018: 111–12)

References

Ballard, J. G. ([1973] 2007), *Concrete Island*, London: Fourth Estate.

Bishop, Elizabeth (1984), *The Complete Poems: 1927–1979*, New York: FSG.

Carpenter, J. R. (2013), '…and by islands I mean paragraphs', *The Island Review*, http://theislandreview.com/content/and-by-islands-i-mean-paragraphs. Accessed 12 June 2020.

Carpenter, J. R. (2015), 'Writing Coastlines: Locating Narrative Resonance in Transatlantic Communications Networks', PhD thesis, Falmouth and London: Falmouth University and University of the Arts London.

Carpenter, J. R. (2018), *An Ocean of Static*, London: Penned in the Margins.

Carpenter, J. R. (2019), 'Writing on the Cusp of Becoming Something Else', in J. Jefferies and S. Kember (eds), *Whose Book Is It Anyway?: A View From Elsewhere on Publishing, Copyright and Creativity*, Cambridge: Open Book Publishers, pp. 243–65.

Carson, Anne (1995), 'The Fall of Rome: A Traveller's Guide', in *Glass, Irony and God*, New York: New Directions, pp. 73–105.

Coetzee, J. M. ([1986] 2010), *Foe*, London: Penguin.

Darwin, Charles ([1838] 1997), *The Voyage of the Beagle*, London: Wordsworth Classics.

Defoe, Daniel ([1719] 2000), *Robinson Crusoe*, Ware: Wordsworth Classics.

Deleuze, Gilles (2004), *Desert Islands and Other Texts, 1953–1974*, Los Angeles: Semiotext(e)/Foreign Agents.

Derrida, Jacques (1978), *Writing and Difference* (trans. A. Bass), Chicago: University of Chicago Press.

Díaz, Hernán (2010), 'A Topical Paradise', *Cabinet 38: Islands*, Brooklyn, New York, pp. 79–85.

Doreski, C. K. (1993), *Elizabeth Bishop: The Restraints of Language*, Oxford: Oxford University Press.

Galloway, Alexander R. (2012), *The Interface Effect*, Cambridge: Polity.

Hayles, N. K. (2006), 'The Time of Digital Poetry: From Object to Event', in A. Morris and T. Swiss (eds), *New Media Poetics: Contexts, Technotexts, and Theories*, Cambridge: MIT Press, pp. 181–210.

Kittler, Friedrich A. (2009), 'Towards an Ontology of Media', *Theory, Culture & Society*, 26:2–3, pp. 23–31.

Lecercle, Jean-Jacques (2002), *Deleuze and Language*, Basingstoke and New York: Palgrave Macmillan.

Lennox, Jeffers (2017), *Homelands and Empires: Indigenous Spaces, Imperial Fictions, and Competition of Territory in Northeastern North America, 1690–1763*, Toronto: University of Toronto Press.

Richter, Gerhard (2007), *Thought-Images: Frankfurt School Writers' Reflections From Damaged Life*, Redwood City: Stanford University Press.

Wark, McKenzie (2011), *The Beach Beneath the Street: The Everyday Life and Glorious Times of the Situationist International*, London and New York: Verso.

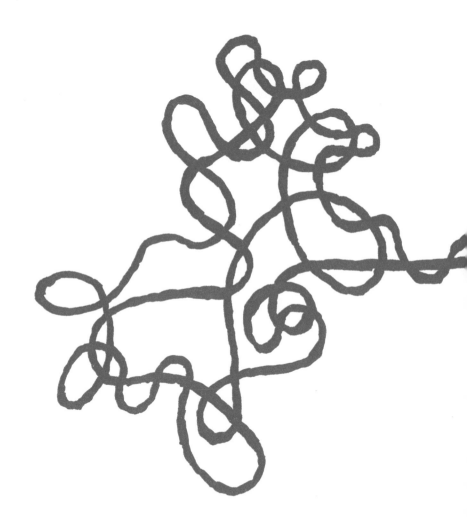

Duet Walk

KAREN CHRISTOPHER AND MARY PATERSON
LED BY KAREN, TRANSCRIBED AND EDITED BY MARY

I have to start by saying, there are these memorials here. They're in beautiful, old style memorial plaques. Each one is written across a number of tiles but they're obviously all you know made for the purpose.

And These are focused on people who sacrificed or died trying to save someone else.

So: Lee Pitt is a 'reprographic operator'. Which has nothing to do with him saving anyone. But you need to know that's what he does because that tells you something about him. 'Aged 30. Saved a drowning boy from the canal at Thamesmead. But sadly was unable to save himself.' And then it says the date.

Then this one. 'Whilst being scolded and burnt ... sacrificed their lives in saving the train.'

And so, it's like that.

And they're quite. I mean, they're quite.

Well no I'm not a foreigner actually because I've been naturalized.
Oh really? How do you know?
How do I know? Because I've got a passport!
Oh – you're an actual citizen!
Yeah, well I wanted to vote, didn't I? So it had to be done.
And that's what being naturalized means, that you get a passport?
You have the right to a passport. You don't automatically get it.
It's a very loaded term.
Isn't that bizarre? I am naturalized! I'm a natural woman!

We are going on a very specific path. So It's really good because they've unveiled it again. It was covered up for a while, while they were restoring it. I'm going to probably forget exactly what it was so I'm going to read on the thing. But It's the union for the guys that made the knives and stuff. Was once upon a time. So let's just see. Be double sure. Yeah, see?

The Worshipful Company of Cutlers.

I never knew that the word cutlery derives from the [reading from a sign] '*Latin cutlarius, from the old French cutellier, a maker or seller of knives and weapons ...*' 'Not simply an artisan but a designer, an assembler of parts, he produced the finished article which he then sold in the market place.'

So! It's Cutler's Hall.

What have you given up in order to work with someone else?

My sanity, my pride, my sense of ownership, my ...! The word I'm looking for, I cannot find. My sovereign will. No!

I can't ...

So all we're doing is we're looking at ... There are some other things further that way but it's too much. I knew it would be. I was really planning to finish right here.

Ok.

There's a plot of land [over there] that belongs to the church, and when you go to it you're in Cambridge or something. You're not here.

Again, it's like the decision to move to London: there's always a self-serving aspect, as well as the difficulty of it, or as well as the giving up of rights and privileges, that has to happen.

I think

in order to

I mean there's a self-sacrifice that has to happen, because of the will of the other person. In as much as my will has to

But when I think about that, I think: it's not really self-sacrifice because I

Want

to do that. Why do I

want to do that?

It was all an accident. It was all really an accident. Well.

I did choose Gerard [Bell].

When I first started this, I figured I needed to start with two people that I chose. So I wrote them letters: one to Stacy Makishi and the other to Gerard Bell. It was a proposition to work together for two weeks. At the end of those two weeks we would decide if we wanted to make a duet together. Stacy and I decided not to. Gerard and I decided to do it.

Sophie [Grodin] asked to be my intern. Because her teacher at Central [School of Speech and Drama] had emailed me and said 'she's my best student', I decided to meet with her to say, 'no', rather than just to say, 'no'. And during the course of the conversation, she was very persistent. And Eventually I found myself suggesting that we could spend the month of her internship as if it's the probationary period for making a duet.

And do you know why they have –
An elephant?
An elephant and a castle?
Nah. I don't know anything about that.
I wonder if it was close to Elephant and Castle. It's the same –
It's the same elephant, and the same bit of castle.
I suppose it's just an elephant that goes into war. [That] is the elephant part of it. And that would make sense because they're selling the swords –
They're doing the sword thing. Their big crest up there has a whole bunch of swords on it.

Because In answering her questions I was describing the process I'd gone through with Stacy and Gerard. And I thought: well, I could do that with you; how does that sound to you? And Teresa [Brayshaw] ... She had known Goat Island. I was at the Flare Festival running a workshop, and her husband is Neil Mackenzie, who runs the Flare Festival, and she came up to me in the lobby. She asked me what I was doing, and I described the duet project to her. I heard myself describing it; and I was describing it better than I ever had before. I was just thinking in my head: wow! it's making sense now.

This is a walk that I did when I first moved here.
So This is just me recreating that walk. Which I've done with other people –
A guided walk?
No, CJ took me.
CJ took you. Did he know where you were going?
Yes.
So, when you first moved to London? Not the first time you visited London?
No.
But when you first moved here?
When I first moved here, when I decided I was going to be living here.
And how did you decide you were going to be living here?
Because: CJ.

Self-sacrifice by giving up *her* lifebelt. Voluntarily going down with the sinking ship.

Trying to save a lad

from dangerous entanglement of weed.

Which is just.

It just stays in my head.

This dangerous entanglement of weed ...   And he was 19 and he was a railway clerk.
And this was July 16th
1876.

And [for] a lot of them There's just one person and the saved person.

They're a series of duets.

Mostly. Not all of them.

But mostly.

One person and another. Doing this thing.

There's nothing to confuse the moment. It's just giving you

a Moment.

In time.

And usually in place.

Then she said, 'I wanna do one with you.

'Can I do one with you?'

Well first of all, Goat Island ended. CJ and I both lived in Chicago, but CJ had been
suffering a little from not being in Britain ... I'm just trying to notice where we are.
The public gallery of ... The court ... Of the Royal Court. Central Criminal court.

Are you being silent because you know it's good
to be silent down here, or is it out of ... No. It's a bit of respect that comes to me. This is
where they come out. Sometimes the press are out here. *Wow.* Trying to catch people.
Sometimes when I go through there and I come out here, there's all press and nothing
happening, or a throng, or like now: not that much.

I can't imagine.
Moving across the world like that.

          I couldn't imagine it either.
          Because the only thing I'd ever wanted in my life
How it feels.   was to stay in one place
To leave that life behind.   and reap the benefits.

          How

      can I proceed in the world and try to be open

      to different ways and a different way of being?

I realized that being in the studio with just one other person was the most terrifying
thing I could do. What I need is a shock!

    where there's no witness. There's no tie breaking person. There's nobody
    who isn't right here. Trying to do this thing. Just you and me. And if I
    don't do something, you're left without someone.   To respond to.

So there was that. And that's what I said. I needed a shock, so that I wouldn't   clearly
not just   so the weight of what to do is equally borne ...

    And This one has complicated language. 'Drowned at Teignmouth whilst trying to
             rescue a boy and baby and seen to be in difficulty.'

                  That. I don't know.

          It just seems like there's a complication there.

How come you were prepared to leave?

I guess because I had made CJ do it. Yeah … I would have just stayed. I would have just stayed.

Jacob Marley's chains! I mean, it's like I have all these performances, from Goat Island, from when I was ten, you know, on, now.

Rattling behind me do you know. They

> they are a lens to see through?
> they have tracked thought patterns in my head?
> they have solidified certain relations that I understand?

I sometimes say a line, by accident, and think: I know that person. Don't you know.

> And they're quite. I mean, they're quite.

My mother used to do these puppet shows. There was a Winnie the Pooh puppet show, and the owl couldn't say the word 'seed' without saying the word 'cake' afterward. So he kept. There was this courtroom scene where he was the judge. He was saying 'this procedure' and he kept saying, 'this proceed-cake'. And now I can't hear the word 'procedure' without saying in my head the word 'cake.'

> It *is* a mental thing. It might be a spiritual thing, if those things are real. Do you
> know? It might be karma, as my mother would like to say. And there's a lot of
> things it could be, but whatever it is, it's a matrix, that holds me there.

What holds me?

And in a strange way I don't feel that I am always right. Or that I always know what the best choice is, or what the best option is. And so Polluting my will with the will of someone else means that I have to really fight. I have to convince the other person. And so If I'm not going to be able to convince them, maybe it's not really a good idea, or not a good idea now, with this other person.

And I didn't say it, because we were crossing the street. And also because you were talking about the piece or the work in front of us, or whatever it is that you actually said. And I think I thought,

that whatever it was we were actually saying deserved to resonate a little bit there rather than me just going to this big thing. But it floated back for some reason

the crossing of the street and everything.

I know that in order to speak to Gerard Bell I have to behave in a certain way, to get the result I want. And so of course I'm manipulating him. He's manipulating me. Responding in a particular way. I am to him. So Everything I come up with is in the context of him. And that's where ownership dissolves; because I can't say anything that I think of is my idea in the absence of Gerard

or the others

Because I think this commitment idea is   easier
        to understand, with just one other person. I mean, for me, in this current period of time that just passed. I think I wasn't sure I could

float

more than one other person. In my commitment requirement.

It's always a dice roll because there's no way to know, from my point of view. Some people know. The press obviously know. They come here. But I have no concept. I have no way of checking. Also, sometimes guys come out with their wigs on, and that's always good for a visitor from the US. If someone says, 'take me on a walk, I'm just visiting,' I say, 'OK!' And I take them here, and it throws them into a swirly tailspin.

That's where the ownership dissolves. I can say – yeah, that was my idea. Of course I can say that. But I would feel wrong not to say the context and the origin and this idea comes as a response to the process of working with *him*. I would never have had the idea otherwise. This would never happen.

I want to be working with people and I want an incredible amount of commitment.

What was I saying?

You were saying, when you worked with Teresa ...

Oh! For instance, I wanted to include something about these moths I'd just read about in a Rebecca Solnit book, *The Faraway Nearby*. There is one story that goes along the bottom edge of all the pages, in a single line. It's about moths that drink the tears of birds. They will actually do it to people, too: eye fluid. They take minerals from it: salt, whatever.

So we're just walking along the river and I say, you know, what I was reading last night, these moths that drink the tears of sleeping birds.

They drink the tears of sleeping birds!

We're walking. And she's just silent. I'm waiting for it to sink in.
It's kind of sinking in.

And then she says. 'But Karen. *Why* are the birds crying?'

(My mother doesn't even remember that. I told her about it, just recently, when she was here, and she was like 'what are you talking about?')

And I was, like

It's about tears.
It's not about anything else.
It's about tears.

This text was commissioned as part of the TwoFold festival of duet performances (2017) and to reflect on TwoFold, which itself reflected on Haranczak/Navarre's duet series, *The Difference Between Home and Poem*.

Resonance of Two

KAREN CHRISTOPHER

A particular configuration in which to think

This is a duet. A duet between you and these words. This is a duet between me from ages ago and you right now. If it is being read aloud to a group of people, this is a duet multiplied. A duet embedded within that duet is between the speaker and these words. And another between those eyes and that mouth.

When I declare it is a duet, I am creating a position, a specific geometry, that includes and excludes, that puts a spotlight on a particular, that establishes a zone of importance or influence. I find the duet form appealing, frightening, engrossing, vexing, irresistible and influential, and I wonder about the origin of the power and intimacy of two.

By making a series of performance duets, I endeavoured to see what the form affords.

Collaborative performance making takes many forms: sometimes there is no director, with all decisions and plans and guidelines arrived at through consensus; sometimes there is a director who facilitates the working process; sometimes that director also performs in the work, sometimes not; sometimes the work begins with a standard theme or focus; sometimes it begins with a search for a focus. What collaborative performance making does not do is start with a completed script to be used as a map or template or put over people like a glove. It is an area of tremendous variability. As part of this, formal constraints, whether practical or aesthetic, exert influence over the process. The conditions and methods of a working process become embedded in the work itself. A working process creates a specific and distinct language. The language that is brought forth in the course of a making process becomes the language with which the work speaks and is the language of transmission to the audience during the performance event.

I have recently been engaged in making collaborative duets on which I have worked with a few different partner artists. On each of these projects, the people involved worked through consensus to create a level playing field between us where listening and contributing material culminated in a completed performance work. What I mean by consensus is interchangeable with what I mean when I talk about agreement. Using either of these words in reference to making performance work I refer to the practicalities of the work: which foot to use and how many times, where to look and how to look. It is less useful to attempt agreement on where the meaning lies and the right and wrong of things – but we can agree on which story to tell and how long to let the water dry before speaking again. We do have to agree which direction to look, but we do not have to see the same things or think about what we see from the same point of view – agreement is always about the practicalities: when we should meet and where and when to start working and how. And we have to agree when to stop making and start showing the work. Furthermore, agreement on decisions made does not necessarily happen without discord in the process, and it does not mean there are not methods of persuasion, influence, bargaining or outlasting the other partner. Agreement is made because the parties feel that continuing together is better than not continuing together. Sometimes, the human with the strongest resolve wins the day. The solid agreement comes without resort to bullying or blackmailing each other and for each party to operate with generosity and tolerance for difference of opinion. This essay describes some distinct qualities I found specific to working in pairs on collaborative duet performance compositions.

I am using the word 'duet' rather than 'duo'. 'Duo' refers to the two individuals involved and the 'duet' is the form of what happens between them – the composition that is the product of their combined effort.

Any form affords a particular quality of attention, a certain comfort level, a distinct geometry of option. A size gives on to this affordance and also a vibration. Just as a shape or a colour can be influential, the framework, the grid, the airspace of a form has an influence on the nature or quality of interaction undertaken within it. Volume or number of individuals involved in a plan dictates the vibration or resonance of the project working conditions. In the end – unless it folds or unravels altogether – every well-made plan conforms to conditions that win out as a result of negotiations or fail to budge after the urge to resist wears out.

Different numbers of people require different metres

What I say and how I say it is a finely calibrated event that depends quite a lot on how many people are present. Even without overt communication, our behaviour is affected by the number of people we are with. Consider the lift: a small room that carries us vertically through tall buildings causing us to be confined with others with whom we have no business or history – nothing in common except that we are traveling through floors of a building. How is it if we are alone with someone in that tiny room and how does it change if just one more enters when the doors open? If I give a public lecture or talk, I am acutely aware that my tone and manner are different for a gathering of six people than for a gathering of 20 or 30. A talk planned for an audience of nine requires recalibration when, on the day, 60 people show up. But if I have only one person in the audience, even if I do not know the person, this is no longer a public talk. It is too intimate for that.

No majority rule, no mitigation between points of view

I have used the duet form as a way of addressing hierarchy in the collaborative making of performance works. Hierarchies arise from interpersonal power dynamics, history, differing experience levels, social conventions (popular behaviours) and individuals' willingness to expose weaknesses or vulnerability or suffer a loss of dignity. Some people think faster or are more assertive or willing to take creative risks than others. If a hierarchical relation diminishes an individual's sense of agency, ideas become fugitive. Loss of agency stifles impulse and the ability to make connections and gives voice to thought. A duet presents the clearest, simplest way of practicing equality with other people – working on it one person at a time. The presentation of the duet itself becomes a model of that levelling for the viewers of the duet composition.

If there is no one to settle disputes, if there is no mitigating voice between opposing positions, then agreement or accommodation might be reached through persuasion or tortuous obstinacy. Or maybe the two people put off the decision for a later time. It is also possible that one of those people has more confidence than the other, and it is also possible that one of them feels that the greater experience or, conversely, the freshness of youth of the other means that one or the other should take a step back. But if there is to be an actual flattening of hierarchy, then, it does not come because the 'winner' of disagreements is the one who is better at arguing or the less tolerant or less afraid of mistakes or more patient. Agreement has to come freely and fairly as a result of one or the other seeing fit to step back. The only way this can happen freely and without resentment is if the climate between the two is already fostering equality. Maintaining a level field calls for constant practice, a high level of attention, and the humility to say let us do it your way and see what happens. Small practices of faith make this possible.

When one of my duet partners Sophie Grodin and I started working together, we had to reckon with a 27-year age difference between us. She was still at university. I was teaching on an MA course at the same institution where she was on a BA course. The age difference between Sophie and me affords a clear view on management of difference that is usually more subtle between people of a similar age. One way to flatten the hierarchy is to honour – even privilege – difference and to value the presence of discord or disagreement. Rather than agree to the same point of view, the agreement becomes about how to keep both.

There are small mechanisms that re-enforce this practice. We were working in English which is my first language but not Sophie's. As part of our work on the project *Control Signal*, we planned to include a portion of the performance text in her first language, Danish. This was to be spoken by me. She had to teach me how to say it. Sophie fancied this incapacity of mine being played out in front of the audience, so we performed a version of me not knowing the text in Danish each time we performed that section. I had to disregard the possibility of memorizing the Danish translation and let Sophie supply those words to me in front of the audience. This demonstration of humility allowed the audience to read me as less experienced in spite of my grey hair. As part of our warm-up, we practiced a clapping pattern. Sophie was much better at it than I was. This became significant. We worked to refrain from making assumptions about what each other was capable of. We listened to each other especially closely during disagreements with an eye towards finding a way to make both of us satisfied with whatever outcome we settled on. This meant that each of us was open to persuasion and said yes to things we might not have otherwise. This meant that we both practiced patience and working with an open mind. It meant being clear about whether I want to win or make work: if I crush my colleague, I will have a broken person to work with.

We sit opposite each other at the table. I want her to have a good idea as much as I want myself to have one. I want to work with someone who is going to make me better, and if my idea is found wanting, we need at least half a chance that she will have one that moves us. If we can spark it, the dynamic between us provides a fuel. Initially, it is heavy going. Let us say we are soggy brained – it is after lunch, we are slow and looking away into the middle distance. It is taking hours. We are trying to write a text that will deliver some information about a particular historical figure. We want to use the events surrounding her life and what happened to her, but it is possible that our audience will not know her or will not have enough context to feel the impact of our material unless we deliver enough information for them to locate the world we are operating within. But we do not want to slow down. We do not want to go to school desks in the middle of a performance. There is a velocity we have to keep up, pressure on the audience, their attention, and if we do not keep up this velocity, their heart rates will fall to a place where we cannot get them back. We also need this velocity ourselves in the studio. We have a text we are working with that is meaningful to us but that has no place in the world of the material we are working with, and yet, it delivers an idea that we like (*the idea that there are unspoken rules a society operates within and if we do not pay attention to them, we can sometimes behave – automatically, without thinking – in ways we do not intend*). So, I say, let us use this text as a template to say what we want to say about our historical figure. We will simply replace key words and write it 'in the style of' the pre-existing text. This idea made no sense to Sophie. Because I am suddenly incensed that she does not understand me (*how is it possible after so many days working together? it feels like a tiny exposure, a disloyalty, an abandonment that is seismically shifting how I feel about working with another person*) and as I am looking to contain some kind of fusion happening within me, I take the page on which the text is written and I prove it will work by doing it for her. I write it by speaking it. And she sees it. She sees it because she is full of attention now and I rise to the occasion because I am also full of attention and full of energy fuelled by the conviction that I can prove it to her – prove my idea will work. And in this moment, preceded by more than two hours agonizing over writing tired expository approaches, we feel a sense of triumph. Each of us has made this possible, it is spark and fuel in an oxygen-rich atmosphere.

Working with someone twisting to the right as I twist to the left actually holds the two of us together in the way that twisting fibres make a rope, giving us enough contradiction to keep us on our toes. I do not experience derailment on my own as much as I do in the presence of another person. This derailment or some form of uncertainty puts our minds on alert. We wake up and experience accelerated thinking, not actually thinking in words but intuiting through sensation, producing through the nervous system a response that we understand only after we have made it. The moment of being misunderstood, of gasping at a dead end after following a misconceived assumption, of feeling alone in the company of another, produces a jump start that wakes up the active mind. Problem solving is instinctive. Being at a loss provokes the instinct to regain solid ground. Working on a duet involves swinging between cultivating careful communication on the one hand and on the other, persuading ourselves to be comfortable with uncertainty.

Working with two is bicameral, a legislative body with two chambers. It is akin to managing to see through a pair of binoculars. Our views are slightly askew by just about the difference between the point of view from my left eye and the one from my right. And it applies to the audience as well: if they are reading us, they are using each of us as a ballast or reference point for the other. Everything we project pings off the other as if checking the connection between us like a computer. The audience is drawing comparisons, is taking exception to one and is feeling a growing allegiance to one or the other. We give each other a context within which the audience compares us. We are seen in relief; we are each other's backdrop. If the group includes more than two, the tendency is for an individual to be spotlighted against a crowd of others.

In interviews with David Sylvester, the British painter Francis Bacon talked about painting portraits. He said that he preferred not to have a live model present while he was painting. He felt he did an injury to them. He painted best from memory or from photographs. He said the presence of the person in the room made him feel like they were being made to suffer. He worried the subject felt his painting did them an injury. It was distracting to commit this perceived injury with their own flesh and breath and blood vibrating in front of him. He became preoccupied with the discomfort of live models. This projection of discomfort interfered with the free ranging of the painter's plans. He talked in terms of sensation. He was painting sensation, painting what could not be seen, invisible forces (Sylvester 2016: 45–49). His portraits contain impossible states of conflation between people and things, with rupture or stretched or twisted heads or bodies and, in the case of his portraits of Pope Innocent X (after a painting by Velasquez), excruciating facial expressions of torment. He needed to be alone for this transaction to take place. I think he was creating a bond with the image itself – a duet with the painting coming into being. He did not want any influence to interrupt his connection with the painting.

I looked at the interviews between Sylvester and Bacon because they are referenced in *The Logic of Sensation* (2003), Gilles Deleuze's analysis of Bacon's work, in which he focuses a chapter on the coupled figures that feature in many of Bacon's paintings.

These figures appear to consist of two entities in collision with each other. Sometimes it is two people, sometimes a person and an object. There is a sense of two entities acting upon each other with shape-changing force. They are mingled by it. They become entangled or enmeshed. In Bacon's paintings, there is violence in the mixing of two.

Deleuze adopts Paul Klee's description of painting: defining its main task as the attempt to render invisible forces visible, closely relating *forces* with *sensation* (Deleuze 2003: 56). Deleuze observes a coupling of two figures in many of Bacon's paintings and describes the communication between their two levels of sensation. Equating sensation with vibration, he suggests that the relationship between these two levels of sensation creates a resonance (45). In some cases, these are two distinct objects whose vibrations create a resonance between them; in others, this resonance is happening between 'crushed bodies included in a single figure' (65). Deleuze observes that this resonance creates a rhythmic coupling that does not admit a third. The presence of a third figure (often as part of a triptych) becomes an attendant whose rhythm remains apart. Deleuze goes on to cite a similar dynamic in written words and music (66–73). This resonance of sensations is also generated in live performance. I relate it to the work that two people do with each other, both in the composition of a duet in the studio and with participation of the audience in the performance.

The resonance of two may be felt as a sensation and an operative part of an artistic notion or theory, but it is also *a physical fact*. The architecture of the human ear produces the perception of a third tone as a result of being exposed to two tones produced outside the ear canal. Upon hearing two tones of different frequencies, a third or a fifth apart for example, the resonance of these two tones within the chamber of the ear kicks off an extra vibration that we experience as sound without there being an external source for its production (Wolfe 2011). The third tone is the difference in frequencies of the two original tones, a 'difference tone', or a 'Tartini tone' – named after violinist and composer Giuseppe Tartini, who discovered, in 1714, that if two related notes were played simultaneously on a violin, a third sound could be heard. Tartini used this phenomenon as a tool for tuning (Encyclopaedia Britannica 2020). Vibration is the key to the difference between a partnership of two and any other number. It is akin to the confrontation of variant sounds, the sounds that make our ears tingle and invent a third.

The quiver is a movement performed in the duet *Control Signal*. When the audience enters the performance space, this movement is already in motion. Performed by me, standing facing front towards the seating bank, just to the left of centre in the performance area, the quiver is a small but insistent action. The performance of it requires a consistent side-to-side motion of the hips which is allowed to spread to the whole torso by dint of it all being connected. That is, nothing else is moved intentionally, but the shoulders and therefore the arms, the knees and therefore the heels are also moving. The performer attempts to keep the head still and the eyes looking straight forward, without appearing to stare at something in particular. The effect is of a physical hum, a purring engine, a constant rattle. It is a small action with a constant rhythm.

Originally, it was composed as a response to the question: What never stops? The composition of the entire piece began with an investigation into lines of electricity, in our bodies and through the air around us. This led to material focused on vibration or pulse and connected to the ways electricity has been used to control unruly people and animals. The quiver takes on various meanings as the piece goes on and is performed a number of times by both performers standing side-by-side or at different positions within the space, but at the beginning of the performance, it stands as a signal that there will be some mysterious, or at least invisible, forces at work. In 'Consider This', an essay by Mary Paterson written in response to *Control Signal*, she refers to the quiver in a number of ways including as 'a body becoming something else' (see p. 61 in this book). Eirini Kartsaki describes it in the introduction to her book *Repetition in Performance*: 'both performers start to shake, to vibrate, to move with control from side-to-side. Grodin and Christopher shake their arms [...] moving as if they do not know they are moving. They both look ahead' (Kartsaki 2017: 3, and recast in 'Staying With the Tremble', her essay in this book: p. 75). The way Sophie's hand closest to me moves at a speed and rhythm that matches mine while her outer arm works at a slower speed and different rhythm sets up a counterpoint to my steady, almost mechanical rattle. We undoubtedly affect each other, but the manifestation of the effect is various and not always predictable nor matching. In some ways, a counterpoint is more productive than a correspondence as it provokes definition of territory or justification of difference or contradiction. The resonance between two vibrations is most engaging when it produces a new element itself. Kartsaki points out that it seems a force is acting upon the two performers. And she highlights that, as she watches, this invisible force begins to act upon her as well (5).

I perform behaviour specific to a duo. I will not behave in the same way when it comes to the performance of tasks if I am alone. Although I may let myself down over and over again without much push, when working in concert with someone else, I will struggle as much as it takes not to let that person down. It is not always possible to succeed, but I will put in as much effort as I can to live up to my part in a combined effort. This is partly to do with pride – an effort to show what I can do; with competition – I can do as well as or better than the other; with compassion – I do not want to fail to satisfy a need; with responsibility – I do not want to break a contract whether tacit or spoken. But it is also to do with the kind of influence people have on one another. The contagion of attitude and diligence and a spirit of work builds a membrane only as strong as the demonstration of commitment to the work by the individuals involved. This is particularly true for a partnership of two. Three or more might pull along a sluggish partner, but if there are only two on the job, a lack of commitment to the work from one member becomes a drag on the energy of the partnership. If they accept the challenge, it means a pressure of attention is working on both parties.

With a group of three or more, there is a dispersal of attention; it is less intimate. Duos are confined in points of focus, whereas with more than two, the points of focus multiply more rapidly. Duets lack access to a high volume of chaos, which requires more simultaneity than two can provide. In larger groups, there is greater affordance for thinking in terms of generalities and mass demonstration. There is a cacophony of vibration once you step from two to three. Two are still distinct from one another, greater numbers blur distinctions and clarity requires careful engineering.

In the pursuit of diminished hierarchies, there is not only interpersonal hierarchy to consider but there is also a hierarchy amongst the material elements of the performance. Mastery of meaning among and across movement, choreography, spoken word, sound, image and dynamism necessitates a greater control over the people, objects and materials in a larger group. More cooperation is summoned – more confinement of individual license to make decisions in a moment, more to consider in terms of planning and action. This applies similarly in studio sessions (both for composition and rehearsal) as well as in performance before an audience. Imagine two of us looking to the right at the same time with our gaze at the same level, moving with the same speed and tension. Multiply that by five and imagine how many different thoughts reside in those ten heads and how many different ways there are to be distracted or less than willing or not quite at full attention.

The reality of getting ten heads to turn in exactly the same way, at the same time, is that those ten heads have been pounded into submission (willingly, most likely) by numerous repetitions and some strenuous insistence on the part of an outside eye. It is not a better or a worse situation, but it has a different history and a different subliminal effect.

Everyone has two bodies

The duet composition sets up a vibration, has its own rhythm, requires keen attention from both parties – it ceases to be a group if either member of the duo looks away, drops out or loses connection – a quality not shared by other denominations. Taking the other eye in the bicameral view, between two parties, there is no witness, no tie-breaking opinion – the account of their meeting is between them alone and each has only their own word for how they came together and what transpired. It is a configuration that demands faith and responsibility, trust and confidence and a willingness to accept the generative force of difference. The intimacy of two affords the possibility of experiencing how entangled the well-being of the other is to the well-being of oneself.

In her book *The Second Body*, Daisy Hildyard suggests that these days everyone has two bodies – the actual flesh body and the body that is in and of the whole world. In the context of a worldwide network of ecosystems, the second body is 'your own literal physical and biological existence' (2017: 25), a global presence that is larger and more fluid than your flesh body – a version of you that is part of everything.

When I began working on duets and searched for a way to think about the form, I worked with the idea of self and other as the guiding principle that governed both my relationship with my collaborator and the two of us with the audience. It seems each single part of the duo can be multiple. Single units are not stable, but like cells, we divide and multiply. If I am here and also everywhere, says Hildyard, then I am responsible for the well-being of the whole:

> Your first body could be sitting alone in a church in the centre of
> Marseille, but your second body is floating above a pharmaceutical plant
> on the outskirts of the city, it is inside a freight container on the docks,
> and it is also thousands of miles away, on a flood plain in Bangladesh, in
> another man's lungs. (Hildyard 2017: 25)

Notions of ecology and the distribution of bodies relate to performance, and these examples help me see that when we are talking about observing bodies in a room, we are reading more than what is readily legible in a conventional sense. In a mass-produced photo book I often gazed into as a child, I particularly remember a series of photos featuring two people standing together. Underneath each of them, the caption read: 'these two form a multitude'. This moved me greatly but I did not really understand why. I liked the idea that two people meant all people. I was thinking about synecdoche, these two people standing in for others the way the hand stands in for the whole body in the phrase 'all hands on deck'. As an adult, when I found the book again, I realized these couples are all male/female couples from different races and ethnicities, and the implication is they could procreate and thus produce a whole race. It was one of those blind spots that protected a notion somehow dear to me but which was beside rather than part of what its source intended. We all can and do create scaffolds for knowing and believing what we wish to know and believe, and we can be fluid with the application of this capacity.

I am thinking with words, I am thinking with my body; if I am in a context, that context is also part of how I am thinking. I am thinking as a member of a duo. I am thinking through a form involving two people. That is a particular way of thinking.

This essay first appeared in *The Routledge Companion to Performance Philosophy*, edited by Laura Cull Ó Maoilearca and Alice Lagaay, London, 2020.

References

Deleuze, Gilles (2003), *Francis Bacon: The Logic of Sensation* (trans. D. W. Smith), London and New York: Continuum.

Encyclopaedia Britannica (2020), 'Giuseppe Tartini', https://www.britannica.com/biography/Giuseppe-Tartini. Accessed 19 December 2020.

Hildyard, Daisy (2017), *The Second Body*, London: Fitzcarraldo Editions.

Kartsaki, Eirini (2017), *Repetition in Performance: Returns and Invisible Forces*, London: Palgrave Macmillan.

Sylvester, David (2016), *Interviews With Francis Bacon*, London: Thames & Hudson.

Wolfe, Joe (2011), 'Tartini Tones and Temperament: An Introduction for Musicians', The University of New South Wales, https://newt.phys.unsw.edu.au/jw/tartini-temperament.html. Accessed 23 August 2018.

Six Practices of Learning Together in Havruta

ORIT KENT

Picture a room with pairs of learners sitting together learning Jewish texts. All of the learners are engaged in text study in *havruta*. Each pair of learners gathers to closely read ancient texts and talk about their meanings. Some pairs converse excitedly, while others sit more quietly, as they puzzle through an idea. Their ideas, questions, sighs, silence and laughter fill the room with the sounds of learning. They are on a shared voyage – to make meaning of Jewish texts together, to become co-creators with their learning partners as they gain insight into the text and themselves and partake in a conversation across generations.

Introduction

As a form of study, *havruta*[1] – text learning in which two people study a text together – has become increasingly popular in a host of venues in the last decade. It has migrated from traditional Jewish learning contexts to many modern arenas such as adult Jewish learning programs, day school and supplementary schools and Jewish professional development programs. In these contexts, people study a range of texts, both ancient and modern. The pairs sit with one another, read the text together, discuss its meaning and, perhaps, explore broader questions about life that the text raises. While *havruta* is most generally used in Jewish contexts, it is sometimes used in other contexts as well where learners' engagement with texts is central. As a form of textual learning, *havruta* offers learners opportunities to foster intellectual, social, ethical and spiritual engagement and, thus, has a great potential for a range of people in different contexts with different learning goals.[2]

---

1. The Aramaic term *havruta* means friendship or companionship and is commonly used to refer to two people studying Jewish texts together. In this article, the term *havruta* refers to both the learning pair and the practice of paired learning. The history of *havruta* as a widespread learning practice in Eastern European yeshivot is subject to scholarly debate. While documents suggest that *havruta* as a form of study has its roots in the sixteenth century, the merit of studying with other people seems to have more ancient precedent in the Babylonian Talmud. See Orit Kent (2008) for a discussion of this issue.

2. See Orit Kent (2010), 'A Theory of Havruta Learning' in the *Journal of Jewish Education* for the original and full version of this article, which contains transcript analysis of *havruta* learning. This article also draws on Orit Kent (2008), 'Interactive Text Study and the Co-Construction of Meaning', where many of the ideas are further elaborated.

In my own research, I have used the lens of educational and learning theories to analyse real-life *havruta* interactions in order to better understand the forces that support rich and meaningful text learning. I ask the following question: what can we learn about text study and learners' meaning-making through a close examination of adults studying classical Jewish texts in one particular *beit midrash*[3] setting?

In the early phases of my research, I conducted a pilot study in order to illuminate some of the rhythms and complexities of *havruta* learning. I identified *havruta* as a complex and potentially powerful Jewish interpretive social learning practice involving norms, phases, moves and stances. It involves social interaction between two human partners and meaning-making efforts involving three partners – two people and the text (Kent 2006).

Through my early research, I found that the *havruta* encounter provides a particularly generative site for studying the ways people make meaning on a moment-to-moment basis through what they read in the text and hear from their partner. I have been particularly influenced by educator and scholar Patricia Carini's definition of meaning-making, which emphasizes that meaning arises through relationship with others – persons or things. In Carini's words, 'Meaning arises through the relationship among things or persons: that mutual reciprocity that occurs in the act of truly "seeing" something' (1979: 15). In *havruta* learning, then, meaning arises through the interaction and relationship of the three partners of *havruta* – the two people and the text. It, therefore, becomes important to pay careful attention to the interactions and relationships between these three partners.

In my next study of many more *havruta* interactions, I developed a theory of *havruta* in one context.[4] This theory reflects a set of six core learning practices in three dynamic pairs that shape the interactions and relationships between the people and between the people and the text.[5]

3. *Beit midrash* literally means 'house of study' and refers to a place where Jews study texts, often in pairs or *havruta*.

4. The research upon which this study is based took place in a modern *beit midrash* for teacher candidates enrolled in a program at Brandeis. This *beit midrash* included women and men studying a range of Jewish texts in *havruta* over a five-week period. See Feiman-Nemser (2006), Holzer (2006) and Kent (2006) for earlier research in this context. For four summers, I collected audio- and videotapes of nine *havruta* pairs in 51 *havruta* sessions in order to analyze how they make meaning of Jewish texts while learning together.

5. I used a grounded theory (Glaser and Strauss 1967; Cutcliffe 2000) approach to identify some of the central practices in which *havruta* partners engage. I then used tools of discourse analysis (Goodwin 1990; Gee 2005) to further probe the contours of these practices and the ways in which they shape the *havruta's* meaning-making process.

In this article, I will present my theory of *havruta* learning. It is not meant to be 'the' definitive theory but one important frame for helping practitioners and scholars better understand this complex learning experience and make it as fruitful an experience as possible.[6] This theory may also be a helpful lens for both studying and elucidating text-based discussions of other kinds of texts in small and larger group settings.

A theory of havruta learning: overview of six practices

When I use the term *havruta*, I am talking about more than a simple strategy for learners to brainstorm together for a few minutes or what is known in language arts classrooms as 'pair and share' (Calkins 2001). I use the term *havruta* to refer to two people working together for some period of time to together make sense of a text. This requires drawing on skills for how to interpret a text *and* how to work with someone else independent of a teacher's direct guidance. In this kind of *havruta*, effort is directed at constructing ideas and also relationships and the ways in which these processes influence each other. Ideally, the two people involved in the *havruta* are responsible for their own learning and for each other's learning. Their success is viewed as interdependent. Furthermore, as there are not just two partners but three – the two people and the text – for meaning-making to occur, there must be interaction not only between the people but also between both of them and the text.

During a *havruta* discussion, participants construct and reconstruct the meaning of the text through their moment-to-moment interactions. While these interactions are highly complex and, in their particularity, may be highly varied, there are key elements to these interactions. Through analysis of *havruta* recordings and informed by an understanding of good *havruta*, I have identified three pairs of core practices in which *havruta* learners engage: (1) listening and articulating, (2) wondering and focusing and (3) supporting and challenging.

In many ways, listening and articulating are the engine that start the *havruta* and keep it going. Most basically, listening means paying attention to and articulating means expressing one's ideas out loud. Listening and articulating are the building blocks of both idea and relationship development in *havruta*. By both listening and

6. My scholarship draws from a number of areas: literary theory and research on text-based learning (e.g. Haroutunian-Gordon 1991, 2009; Langer 1990, 1995; Scholes 1985; Iser 1978; Rosenblatt 1978), research on peer learning (e.g. Cohen 1994; Cohen et al. 2002; Johnson and Johnson 1989, 1999; Johnson et al. 1996) and research on classroom discourse (e.g. Barnes and Todd 1995; Cazden 1988, 2001; Michaels et al. 2008; O'Connor and Michaels 1996). Underlying my work are assumptions drawn from sociocultural theories of knowledge (e.g. Lave and Wenger 1991; Rogoff 1990; Vygotsky 1978).

articulating, *havruta* partners create space for each human partner and the text to be heard and be part of the *havruta* learning process. This back and forth opens up room for new ideas to emerge, for shaping and refining ideas on the table and for developing a learning relationship.

The second pair of practices is wondering and focusing: being curious and exploring multiple possibilities and concentrating attention. A *havruta* needs to wonder in order to generate creative ideas. At the same time, a *havruta* needs to be able to focus in order to deepen an interpretation and come to some conclusion about the meaning of the text. While listening and articulating are the engine, wondering and focusing are part of the steering wheel – they help determine the direction that the conversation will take.

And finally, there are the practices of supporting and challenging. Both of these practices can help a *havruta* further shape their ideas, but each does so in a slightly different way. Supporting consists of providing encouragement for the ideas on the table and helping further shape them by clarifying them, strengthening them with further evidence and/or, sometimes, extending them. Challenging consists of raising problems with ideas on the table, questioning what is missing from them and drawing attention to contradictions and opposing ideas. These practices also help steer the conversation and can help the *havruta* partners sharpen their ideas.

These six practices are operational not just between people but also between people and the text. For example, learners listen to the text, paying attention to its many details and gaps. While the text is different than a person in that it relies on human beings to give it voice and articulate, it too is a subject in the *havruta* learning process. As one *havruta* learner commented, 'When I'm wrong about my idea, the text proves me wrong'. By closely listening to the text and letting its articulations interact with our own, the text can both support and challenge our ideas.

In order to have a *havruta* conversation of any kind that is more than just parallel monologues, the six practices must take place in some kind of balance. The exact balance will differ from pair to pair, interaction to interaction and even moment to moment and will help determine the result of the *havruta* interaction. The practices in each pair are, on the surface, mutually exclusive. For example, to focus on an idea, one must put aside thoughts of other paths not taken. However, one can never fully stop the practice of wondering or else one runs the risk of discussing stagnant ideas. A tension inheres within each pair of practices in trying to strike some sort of balance between them – a tension that can make *havruta* interactions dynamic, undetermined, hard and potentially engaging.

These practices are best supported in a learning environment that fosters collaboration. This does not mean that everyone needs to agree. A collaborative environment is one in which students understand that their success as a *havruta* is interdependent and that they are, therefore, responsible to and for one another. Furthermore, such a context places a high value on participants working together to develop the most compelling ideas possible and not simply sticking with one's own original idea at the expense of all else.

A closer look at the six learning practices

In what follows, I further define the six practices and their interplay. In an actual *havruta*, the practices are often interwoven, but for the purposes of illustrating them clearly, it is useful to artificially separate them.

Listening and articulating

There are a number of different ways that *havruta* partners listen to one another: listening to follow along, listening to understand, listening to figure something out and listening to witness. Listening to follow along means that one focuses on hearing the other's words in order to keep up and not lose the place. (Sometimes, the objective in listening to follow along is to gear up for one's own turn, though that runs the risk of not really listening while one mostly waits out the other person until one can articulate.) Listening to understand is different from listening to follow along. When one *havruta* partner tries to understand the other's ideas, the partner moves the other from an object of attention to a subject in their own right. To understand the other, one needs to practice both outer and inner silence – creating an outer space for the other to articulate and also silencing the many internal voices that arise in one's own heads so as to truly pay attention to what the other is trying to say (Waks 2008). Listening to understand goes a long way to helping *havruta* members feel respected and also to making sure that different perspectives and questions get raised and responded to. *Havruta* learners may also listen for the purpose of figuring something out – perhaps to figure out a puzzle in the text such as the character's motivations. And finally, *havruta* learners may listen for the purpose of giving their partner space to share and explore an interpretation and to be a witness to their partners' emerging ideas. This kind of listening requires an inner stillness and an alertness to the other and the ability to be fully present to another in the moment.

Havruta learners engage in two types of articulations: exploratory articulations and definitive articulations. Exploratory articulations have the quality of thinking out loud. In addition to inviting one's partner into one's thinking, this kind of articulating can also help people work through their own idea. The more they talk, the more they get clearer on what they are actually thinking and wanting to say. The second type of articulating, definitive articulation, is stating one's idea. Although it is often an important goal of *havruta* learning that learners get to the point of being able to share an interpretation of the text with one another and work that through, it is also key that they leave open space for alternative ideas to emerge, whether from the text and/or their human partner. Learners, therefore, need to balance their types of articulations, creating a context for their *havruta* work to keep drawing on the interpretive resources all partners bring to the table, even as the conversation progresses and begins to focus on certain interpretive ideas.

Through their back and forth between listening and articulating, *havrutot* (multiple pairs of students; this word is the plural of *havruta*) develop a respectful working relationship while increasing the 'interactivity' (Elbow 1986) of their various ideas. Taking turns listening and articulating is slow and hard work – it entails focusing on the other person and the text, restating the other's ideas and building on those ideas further. However, by taking turns in this way, *havruta* partners bring each other and the text into the conversation and can create a sense of respectful dialogue in which all parties' ideas have space to be articulated and heard. They also create a space of interactivity – a space in which ideas get bounced about, rubbed up against one another, elaborated or discarded – and in such a space, there is the potential for fresh insights.

Wondering and focusing

When *havruta* learners wonder, they are curious about the meaning of the text or the meaning of their human partner's interpretation. They generate multiple ideas, questions and/or 'noticings' about the interpretation at hand. Wondering entails asking many questions, most basically, 'What does this mean?'

There can be an open-ended, unbounded kind of wondering in which *havrutot* are drawn to notice different ideas and parts of the text. This kind of wondering can go in many different directions and allows the *havruta* to think out loud and generate new hypotheses and insights about the text, which may or may not connect or might even contradict each other. This kind of wondering seems to allow partners to take hold of the text in their own ways, sparking a certain level of creative energy that helps fuel and refuel the *havruta* interaction.

When *havruta* learners focus, they can concentrate their attention in any number of ways: on the text, on their partner's idea and/or on a particular question. Focusing gives *havrutot* an opportunity to deepen an initial idea and try to work it through.

The unstated and even unconscious dilemma is that if the *havruta* wonders in too many directions and does not shift to focus, it will end up *wandering* and not move forward with any one idea. At the same time, if *havrutot* do not wonder, they often get carried away by unexplored and underdeveloped first impressions. In generative *havruta* discussion, focusing on a way of understanding the text occurs in a dynamic relationship with wondering about the meanings of the text.

Often, wondering is motivated by the fact that there is a space or gap in the text or their partner's idea that engages the learners. Wolfgang Iser (1978) writes that textual gaps engage readers, as the reader is driven to try and fill the gaps in order to make sense of the text. In this way, wondering about gaps pulls the conversation forward. As this occurs, learners may develop an overarching question (or what Sophie Haroutunian-Gordon [1991] calls their 'genuine issue'), which keeps them engaged with each other and the text and creates a purpose to their conversation. The result is that the wondering is not wandering but allows learners to build a more and more comprehensive interpretation. This is a kind of focused wondering framed by their question, with a focus that is sustained and probed over time as learners return to the text and one another to address their overarching question.

The interplay between wondering and focusing helps *havrutot* delve more deeply into the text and consider different ways of understanding the text. It is important for *havrutot* to take time to focus and pursue particular interpretations, while maintaining a sense of curiosity toward new meanings and ideas that might emerge from the text. This is the dance of wondering and focusing. It requires a complicated stance – moving towards closure, while simultaneously maintaining curiosity and openness to new ideas.

Supporting and challenging

Supporting in this context means further developing ideas that are on the table. This can entail several different moves. One is to build on each other's ideas. By building on one's partner's ideas, one sends a signal that these are good ideas and worth working on together. Another type of supporting comes in the form of making explicit moves to help one's partner develop their idea. This comes in the form of asking questions about one's partner's interpretation or the text that creates space for them to think some more, clarify their ideas and flesh them out further. Explicit supporting moves also come in the form of offering supporting evidence for one's partner's idea.

These types of supporting moves are focused on the ideas and the thinking and not the person. This is important. The point of offering support is not that one likes or dislikes one's partner, or even necessarily likes or dislikes their ideas, but that one is committed to helping develop the richest interpretations possible. Even if one does not agree with one's partner (at least at first), one can still support them in making their ideas stronger. In the process of doing so, one may gain insight into their partner's ideas or even their own.

Challenging in this context means noticing the limitations of ideas and holding them accountable to evidence. There are two main types of challenging that we see in *havruta*. First, there is a direct form of challenging in which the partners say things like 'Is this idea supported by the text?', 'What are the limitations of this idea?' or 'How would this idea stand up under this particular hypothetical situation?' There is another type of challenging, a more implicit type of challenging in which one of the *havruta* partners simply suggests an alternative reading. The weakness of implicit challenges is that they can go unnoticed and, therefore, not have an impact on the larger discussion.

As with the supporting moves, when a *havruta* makes a constructive challenging move, the challenge is not to the other person but to the idea, and the challenger does not need to disagree with the idea in order to challenge it or wonder about a possible weakness in it. The point of the challenging is to be able to help each other step back and think through ideas: Are these ideas supported by the text? How does this interpretation stand in the face of alternative interpretations? In this way, *havruta* partners can help one another develop the strongest possible interpretations. Constructive challenging is very different than debating, in which the goal is to win by making points that are often at the expense of one's colleagues. The goal of constructive challenging within *havruta* is to work with one's human partner to notice the limitations of the ideas on the table and refine them. When effective, challenging can help a *havruta* come up with a better articulated interpretation, a more all-encompassing idea or a new idea altogether.

Havruta partners engage in both listening and articulating in order to access the text and their own thinking and bring themselves and the text into relationship to develop interpretations. They engage in wondering and focusing and challenging and supporting to explore the text and their interpretations and expand their fields of meaning, while further refining their understandings. As they engage in learning, they must make many decisions in the moment – Should I listen now and to what and for what? Should I share my new insight even though it is not fully formed? Should I let my *havruta* partner keep sharing their idea? Should I focus attention on that particular idea and pursue it further? Should I brainstorm new ways to consider this part of the text? Should I jump in to challenge my partner's idea with another perspective or simply to reinforce their perspective, as there is a part that I agree with? These are some of the questions the *havruta* partners might consider, consciously or unconsciously, as they move through their *havruta* discussion.

These decision points highlight the need for *havruta* learners to seek to balance their use of the six learning practices. For example, while it is important for a *havruta* to engage in supporting, too much supporting with little challenging can lead to uncritical affirmation. Too much challenging with little support also has its risks. In such a case, a *havruta* can easily enter a never-ending cycle of debating, in which they simply take stands rather than exploring ideas. Finally, little challenging with little supporting can lend itself to a static discussion, in which each person puts forth their ideas without benefiting from interplay with their partner's thinking. Rather, it is in the balance of these practices that the potential of *havruta* can be realized.

It is important to keep in mind that while *havruta* as a learning structure holds much potential for learning, it is not a panacea. It must be used in relationship to specific learning goals and scaffolded for particular students in order to make it 'educative' (Dewey [1938] 1997: 37) and maximize its learning potential.

Through their listening and articulating, their wondering and focusing, their supporting and challenging, *havruta* partners can create the space to notice and respond to one another and the text; they can develop a responsive space. It is in such a space that we begin to see and relate not only to ourselves and our own ideas but also to others – in this case, to our peer partners and the text. And it is through this process of heightened seeing and relating that we can create meaning (Carini 1979). Perhaps it is the power of this responsive space to which the Talmud alludes when it tells us that when two people listen to each other when studying halakhah,[7] the Shekhinah – God's essence on earth – listens to them.

Addendum

Since this article was originally published, I, along with my colleagues, have built on these ideas through both continued research and practice. Allison Cook and I have developed an approach to teaching a learning that is in part based in this framework and is called the Pedagogy of Partnership (PoP). Teachers and learners have used this framework and PoP to help guide learning relationships in many different kinds of contexts and grouping structures. We have seen over and over again in practice that learners get better at this kind of learning and engagement when they are intentionally taught the skills and attitudes represented in this framework, and the use of the practices is not simply left to chance.

We have heard from people around the globe that they have found this framework useful for naming processes that often get unnamed, for it is only by naming them that we can begin to intentionally use them and get better at them. Teachers of math, science, history and literature are using this framework, alongside teachers of Jewish texts, to deepen student learning. Educators have also used this framework to support work with a much expanded notion of what constitutes a text, which includes, for example, photos, videos and personal stories. School staff and faculty are also using this framework to improve their own communications and collaborations. The framework – and tools we have developed for their skillful use – has made their way into other workplace contexts and playground and family interactions as well.

Through the use of the six practices framework in many contexts, we have come to understand it as a learning framework that can support relational learning broadly. The pandemic has only strengthened this understanding, as we have seen educators use this framework to successfully support relationship building and learning online. Even as the world changes, the human need and capacity for relationships – and for frameworks and tools to cultivate those relationships – are enduring.

---

7. Halakhah refers to legal material, in contrast to aggadah, the non-legal material in the Talmud.

References

Barnes, Douglas and Todd, Frankie (1995), *Communication and Learning Revisited: Making Meaning Through Talk*, Portsmouth: Heinemann.

Calkins, Lucy (2001), *The Art of Teaching Reading*, New York: Longman.

Carini, Patricia (1979), *The Art of Seeing and the Visibility of the Person* (ed. North Dakota Study Group on Evaluation), North Dakota: University of North Dakota Press.

Cazden, Courtney (1988), *Classroom Discourse: The Language of Teaching and Learning*, Portsmouth: Heinemann.

Cazden, Courtney (2001), *Classroom Discourse: The Language of Teaching and Learning*, 2nd ed., Portsmouth: Heinemann.

Cohen, Elizabeth (1994), 'Restructuring the Classroom: Conditions for Productive Small Groups', *Review of Educational Research*, 64:1, pp. 1–35.

Cohen, Elizabeth, Lotan, Rachel, Abram, Percy, Scarloss, Beth and Schultz, Susan (2002), 'Can Groups Learn?', *Teachers College Record*, 104:6, pp. 1045–68.

Cutcliffe, John (2000), 'Methodological issues in grounded theory', *Journal of Advanced Nursing*, 31:6, pp. 1476–84.

Dewey, John ([1938] 1997), *Experience and Education*, New York: Simon & Schuster.

Elbow, Peter (1986), *Embracing Contraries*, New York: Oxford University Press.

Feiman-Nemser, Sharon (2006), '*Beit Midrash* for Teachers: An Experiment in Teacher Preparation', *Journal of Jewish Education*, 72:3, pp. 161–83.

Gee, James (2005), *An Introduction to Discourse Analysis, Theory and Method*, New York: Routledge.

Glaser, Barney and Strauss, Anselm (1967), *The Discovery of Grounded Theory: Strategies for Qualitative Research*, New York: Aldine de Gruyter.

Goodwin, Charles (1990), 'Conversation Analysis', *Annual Review of Anthropology*, 19, pp. 283–307.

Haroutunian-Gordon, Sophie (1991), *Turning the Soul, Teaching Through Conversations in the High School*, Chicago: University of Chicago Press.

Haroutunian-Gordon, Sophie (2009), *Learning to Teach Through Discussion: The Art of Turning the Soul*, New Haven: Yale University Press.

Holzer, Elie (2006), 'What Connects "Good" Teaching, Text Study and *Hevruta* Learning? A Conceptual Argument', *Journal of Jewish Education*, 72:3, pp. 183–205.

Iser, Wolfgang (1978), *The Act of Reading: A Theory of Aesthetic Response*, Baltimore: John Hopkins University Press.

Johnson, David and Johnson, Roger (1989), *Cooperation and Competition: Theory and Research*, Edina, MN: Interaction Book Company.

Johnson, David and Johnson, Roger (1999), *Learning Together and Alone: Cooperative, Competitive, and Individualistic Learning*, 5th ed., Boston: Alyn and Bacon.

Johnson, David, Johnson, Roger and Smith, Karl (1996), *Academic Controversy: Enriching College Instruction Through Intellectual Conflict*, ASHE-ERIC Higher Education Report, 25:3, Washington, DC: The George Washington University, Graduate School of Education and Human Development.

Kent, Orit (2006), 'Interactive Text Study: A Case of *Hevruta* Learning', *Journal of Jewish Education*, 72:3, pp. 205–33.

Kent, Orit (2008), 'Interactive Text Study and the Co-Construction of Meaning: *Havruta* in the DeLeT *Beit Midrash*', PhD dissertation, Waltham: Brandeis University.

Kent, Orit (2010), 'A Theory of *Havruta* Learning', *Journal of Jewish Education*, 76:3, pp. 215–45.

Langer, Judith (1990), 'The Process of Understanding: Reading for Literary and Informative Purposes', *Research in the Teaching of English*, 24:3, pp. 229–60.

Langer, Judith (1995), *Envisioning Literature: Literary Understanding and Literature Instruction*, New York: Teachers College Press.

Lave, Jean and Wenger, Etienne (1991), *Situated Learning, Legitimate Peripheral Participation*, New York: Cambridge University Press.

Michaels, Sarah, O'Connor, Catherine and Resnick, Lauren (2008), 'Deliberative Discourse Idealized and Realized: Accountable Talk in the Classroom and in Civic Life', *Studies in Philosophy and Education*, 27:4, pp. 283–97.

O'Connor, M. C. and Michaels, Sarah (1996), 'Shifting participant frameworks: Orchestrating thinking practices in group discussion', in D. Hicks (ed.), *Discourse, Learning and Schooling*, New York: Cambridge University Press, pp. 63–103.

Rogoff, Barbara (1990), *Apprenticeship in Thinking*, Oxford and New York: Oxford University Press.

Rosenblatt, Louise (1978), *The Reader, the Text, the Poem: The Transactional Theory of the Literary Work*, Carbondale: Southern Illinois University Press.

Scholes, Robert (1985), *Textual Power, Literary Theory and the Teaching of English*, New Haven: Yale University Press.

Vygotsky, L. S. (1978), *Mind in Society: The Development of Higher Psychological Processes*, M. Cole, V. John-Steiner, S. Scribner and E. Souberman (eds), Cambridge: Harvard University Press.

Waks, Leonard (2008), 'Listening from Silence: Inner Composure and Engagement', *Paideusis*, 17:2, pp. 65–74.

Introductory Fragment 2: Heart and Lungs

KAREN CHRISTOPHER

An essential element of a live performance event is the creation of a joint experience – everyone in the room goes somewhere. We may not all go to the same 'place', but we go there together. We are soaking in the moment, in each moment, nestled as it is, between the moment fading and the next one showing up.

At the start of an event, one way to bring everyone in is to take away the formality of strangeness. If I am in a position to address the assembled house directly, either by speaking to one of them publicly or all of them intimately, this opens a path of direct access. It puts a light on the difference between, on the one hand, *we all sit in the dark and pretend we are eavesdropping* and, on the other, *we recognize that some of us here prepared something to show to the rest of us who will now allow some time for that.*

It is a pact best made by example or inference rather than by decree. If there are latecomers, it is easily done – it is a bit of a sly trick to refer to latecomers quite overtly and to say 'let's start again from the beginning so as not to leave them out – or would anyone like to get them up to speed?' It is a game – it is playful – it is saying we take all comers even if they are causing a ruffle. We use that ruffle and highlight it as a way of diffusing the sense that some of us are more here just because we were on time. The tacit by-product of this is that we are all now thinking about ourselves as a group. We are all here.

These manoeuvres are tricky because they can fall flat. They fall flat when they smell like fear, when they seem desperate. But if it is simply offered as one of the possible realities taking place right now, and one which we can position as we choose, then it is simply part of what we came here to do and it is unlikely to fall apart unless we look away – which is to say, give up on cooperation.

In some ways, cooperation is at the heart of everything I think about or do. The cooperation between two is a distinctly precarious proposition because there is no 'following the crowd' to avoid the responsibility of holding up your own end of the decision-making moment.

Why do we have two lungs and only one heart? Some questions are more to make us think than to be answered. Sometimes, the answer is less interesting than the thought process the question provokes.

We have two eyes, most of us, if we can see, we can see with one eye well enough, but if we see with two eyes, we have the advantage of depth perception. Two means more than one input synthesized into a version of what we are looking at. We did have two hearts when we were in the embryonic stage. Before we were born, these two fused together into one heart with four chambers.

Consider This (Control Signal)

MARY PATERSON

Consider this: you are seated in a dark room in front of a dark stage, gazing over the dark shapes of other people's heads, and you are aware, ever so slightly, of a prickly irritation caused by the nasal hum of someone else's breathing just as you can feel, ever so slightly, your neighbours' neck muscles tense each time you scratch your pencil across a page in your notebook, and you begin to hear a noise that sounds like air being released from a tyre or pressure escaping from an industrial machine, and this noise is coming from the direction of the stage but you cannot see exactly from where, so you lift your pencil from your notebook and crane your neck up and over the dark shapes of other people's heads and you hear the crackle of a raincoat behind you, which means that someone else is doing the same, and you look into the dark shadows of the stage until you see her: crouched at the front, a woman in a utilitarian pinafore that is reminiscent of a nurse's uniform or a manual worker's uniform or some other type of clothing that denotes a role more than it dresses an individual, and she is expelling her breath through her mouth, which is held very wide and very open, just as you might hold your mouth if you were going to expel a loud breath onto a piece of silverware before rubbing it to a shine with a soft cloth, and in between each breath, this utilitarian woman takes a brush and sweeps a dusty material onto the floor, a material which, you realize after twisting your neck some more, is sticking to the warm, moist residue of her rhythmic exhalations, and you realize that the noise you heard, without knowing where it came from, is the sound of this woman using the alchemy of her breath to coax a line of powder, incrementally, across the stage, which is to say: to make something appear from nothing.

Consider this: you are seated in a dark room in front of a mostly dark stage and you see a woman whose feet are planted in a pair of practical boots while the rest of her body shakes loosely and thoroughly above them; loosely and thoroughly but slowly at first and then faster and more vigorously until you can hear the sounds of her fingers slamming into one another as they vibrate at the ends of her hands, which vibrate at the ends of her wrists, which vibrate at the ends of her arms, which vibrate at the ends of her shoulders, her collarbone, her neck, her head, as if she is a marionette puppet being handled carelessly from above or, alternatively, as if she is some kind of an element being driven by a force that emanates from the centre of her body or, as you think later, when you have seen other things happen on this stage (like an elephant dance slowly and sadly in a black and white film and two train carriages roll endlessly on separate tracks and a political prisoner being executed in an American jail, even though none of these things appear in this mostly dark room, which is to say, these things appear but they are not materially present) that she shakes like a body that is becoming something else, that as her face dissolves into a blur and her limbs begin to rattle, that this utilitarian woman is being transformed into a different person, vessel, character or machine, which is to say, at this moment in time, she is all these things simultaneously: the possibility of all the lives she could lead, all the memories she could inhabit, all the people she is not and all the places she will ever be.

Consider this: you are seated in a mostly dark room, and for the third time in a period that you would measure in minutes rather than hours, two women have turned dramatically towards you and other people like you and announced with grand clarity, as if they are rolling the words around in their mouths to discover exactly what they are made of, that they will Now Synchronize Their Hearts, and they trace a finger across each other's chests as if drawing out the movement of each other's organs with some kind of elemental force or transference that emanates from the centres of their bodies, and you almost feel your own heart pause for half a beat in order to be synchronized too, and you know with the part of your mind that is irritated by the presence of your neighbours' untidy bodies that the hearts of these two women do not beat in unison following the tracing of their fingers, just as you know that they are not an elephant dancing slowly and sadly in a black and white film and they are not two train carriages rolling endlessly on separate tracks and they are not a woman who died when a plume of smoke left her body, and in fact, the appearance of all these things onstage is a kind of showmanship, a leap of faith taken voluntarily in the dark like the time the two women turn to us and toast us with their cups of water, the same water that has washed the hands of everyone here, or that has appeared to, which they lift to their mouths as if it is a rare and expensive substance that should only be enjoyed in company, and just as, when the two women trip the moment before the liquid reaches their lips, spilling the water at the feet of the people seated in the front row and thereby letting real water seep dangerously close to real bodies, and not just the appearance of all these things, just as in that moment you know that a picture of conviviality has been shattered, so you are sure, when you watch the hearts synchronize for the third time, that you and the people like you are all pretending, in other words that this is a pretence, the artifice of which we have individually and collectively chosen to ignore in favour of a leap into showmanship, unison and the appearance of something from nothing, which is to say: we are comforted by magic.

Consider this: not long ago you saw two hands waving, two palms carving through the air as if the air was heavy as smoke and dark as matter, as if the movement of the hands could whip the air into a kind of thickness, and at that time you thought about the shapes of the heads in front of you and the bodies you have left in the foyer and the person sitting behind you who is wearing a coat that crackles when she turns, and at that time you admired the smooth uniformity of the movement across two hands that belonged to two women born half a generation apart, smooth and sure like a slow and accomplished dance, and you could see from the concentration on the faces of the women whose hands were moving that the carving of their palms through the air clasped something grave and important to itself, but it is only now, a period of time later that you would measure in minutes, if you were counting, which you are not, even quietly to yourself in that muted part of your brain that searches for order in things like a body searches for another body in a busy street, it is only now that you have seen other things appear on this stage that you realize this smooth and sure movement that whips the air into a thickness is also a spell that summons the traces of a plume of smoke that has risen from the head of a woman who was strapped to a chair in a room which may or may not have been dark, while a current was administered by hands and bodies that were not her own and passed through her skin, forced through her nerves, pushed through her synapses, until her limbs convulsed and her fingers slammed loudly into one another and something left: a plume of smoke, just like this one, or in fact exactly this one, which has been summoned here, in a movement which you admired at first for its beauty and accomplishment, and which you feel keenly now because it is elemental and real in a way that is not materially real but really present nonetheless, a reality whipped into the air with a simple and repeated movement until the room is thick with the memory of a stranger who tickles the hairs on the back of your neck, which is to say: our bodies do not keep us apart.

'To be lost', says the woman in a utilitarian pinafore reminiscent of a uniform given to a prisoner or to a school girl or of the bland attire of a member of the chorus, 'is to walk in small circles around yourself', and it is in that moment, when the woman looks up from the line of powder being coaxed across the floor by her loud and invisible breath and turns her eyes to her companion on the stage, a woman born half a generation apart who is dressed in the same, drab style that standardizes the bodies of these two people in a manner that also draws attention to their expressive and particular faces, that you wonder just how long it is that you have been lost, and you realize just why your body felt so heavy as you watched the two women transform themselves, recently, into a pair of train carriages that roll endlessly on separate tracks, their eyes turned inwards until their faces became masks reminiscent of the gap between the version of yourself you present to the world and the version of yourself that you long to be understood, and you begin to wonder if you will ever be the kind of person who could vibrate until her fingers shook and whether, if you were that kind of person, you would be shaking out of fear, loneliness, persecution caused by a mistaken belief in the separation of bodies or comfort borne from the potential of change or, in other words, for something to arise from nothing and return to nothing again like the vibrations of a train carriage that career through the ground for hundreds of miles to rattle the seat of a man who is no longer alive.

Consider this: there was once an elephant that was made to perform; there was once a woman called Ethel who died for something she may or may not have believed in; there was once a person who went looking in the city; there was once a dark room lined with the shapes of other people's heads; there was once a body that convulsed when it was struck by lightning, electrical current or elemental force; there was once a pair of hearts that beat in unison, a pair of arms that waved in time, a pair of hands that were washed ceremoniously in front of a group of people just like you, as if they could have been your hands, as if they held the potential to slip into the fingers of all hands like so many pairs of human gloves; but, for a moment, you must try to forget almost all of these things because you cannot wrap your palm around the great sum of possibilities they entail and you cannot keep staring into the shadows or straining for the answer to a mysterious noise, or else you will never leave this dark room, and more importantly, you will forget to remember the expressive and particular details of anything in particular, for example, the expressive and particular details of a skeleton of a chair that is levitating on a stage, that is lifted by the taut power of two ropes held by the bodies of two women who are walking in unison in opposite directions, so that the seatless chair twists and turns slowly above the stage like an animal trained to act against its nature in order to meet the expectations of another species unable, unwilling or uneducated to imagine the gulf of understanding between their kind and its kind, an acceptance which, if it had been gained, might coax the two parties towards the recognition of some thing or some things they might have in common, which is to say: might synchronize their hearts.

Mary Paterson saw *Control Signal*
on 10 October 2013, at Chelsea Theatre, London.

Images from Haranczak/Navarre Performance Projects' duet series

The following pages include performance photographs documenting work from the duet series produced by Haranczak/Navarre Performance Projects. The middle two-page spread shows excerpts from an audience leaflet offering information about source material from the duet *Control Signal*.

The studio performances were most often played to small audiences in spaces where we could hear everyone breathing and their clothes rustling in the quiet bits. This work was made on an intimate scale with attention and space for the performer–audience relationship.

The outdoor piece, *Seven Falls*, was performed for both assembled and accidental audiences at each of its performance sites. In the photo on the last page of the spread, we performers are waving to a sailing ship just choosing this perfect moment, with our arms raised to Cardiff Bay, to set sail and leave. We fancied the possibility that the assembled audience might have thought we had carefully choreographed that moment.

Figure 1, opposite:
miles & miles
Karen Christopher & Sophie Grodin

Figures 2 & 3:
So Below
Gerard Bell & Karen Christopher

Figures 4 & 5:
Seven Falls
Teresa Brayshaw & Karen Christopher

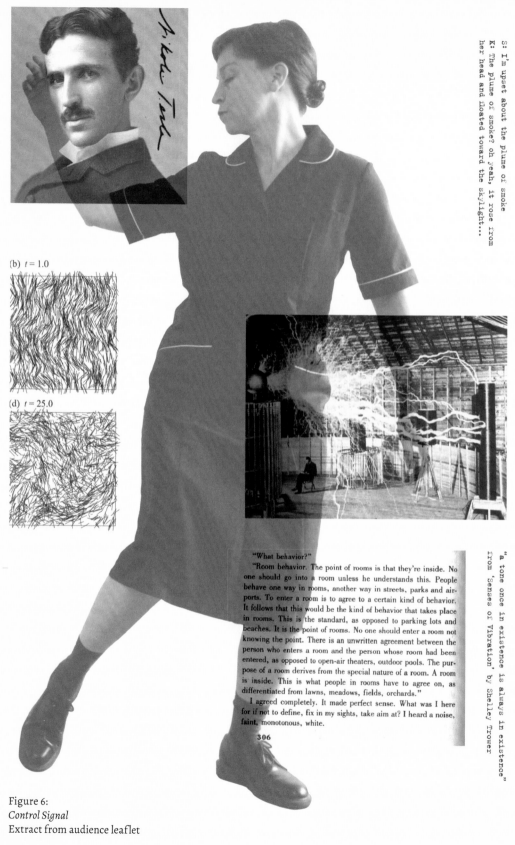

(b) *t* = 1.0

(d) *t* = 25.0

S: I'm upset about the plume of smoke
K: The plume of smoke? oh yeah, it rose from
her head and floated toward the skylight...

"What behavior?"

"Room behavior. The point of rooms is that they're inside. No one should go into a room unless he understands this. People behave one way in rooms, another way in streets, parks and airports. To enter a room is to agree to a certain kind of behavior. It follows that this would be the kind of behavior that takes place in rooms. This is the standard, as opposed to parking lots and beaches. It is the point of rooms. No one should enter a room not knowing the point. There is an unwritten agreement between the person who enters a room and the person whose room had been entered, as opposed to open-air theaters, outdoor pools. The purpose of a room derives from the special nature of a room. A room is inside. This is what people in rooms have to agree on, as differentiated from lawns, meadows, fields, orchards."

I agreed completely. It made perfect sense. What was I here for if not to define, fix in my sights, take aim at? I heard a noise, faint, monotonous, white.

306

"a tone once in existence is always in existence"
from 'Senses of Vibration' by Shelley Trower

Figure 6:
Control Signal
Extract from audience leaflet

68

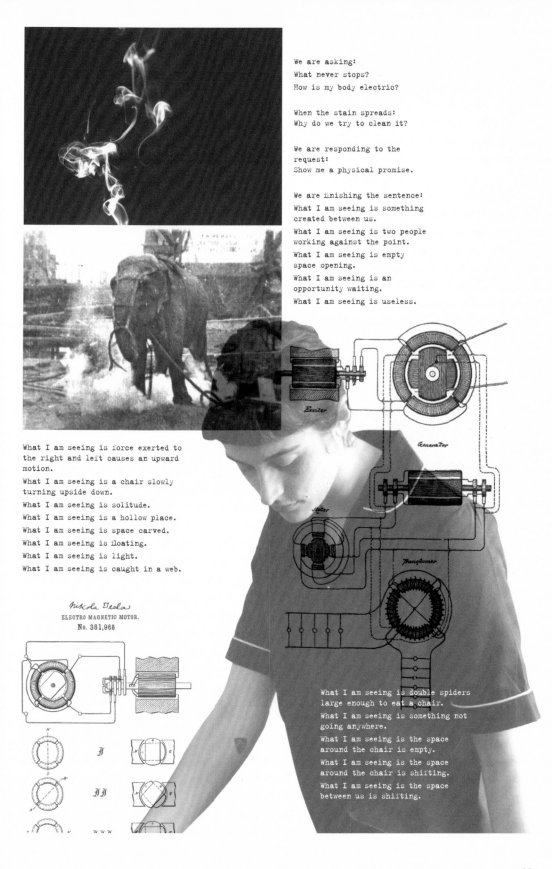

We are asking:
What never stops?
How is my body electric?

When the stain spreads:
Why do we try to clean it?

We are responding to the
request:
Show me a physical promise.

We are finishing the sentence:
What I am seeing is something
created between us.
What I am seeing is two people
working against the point.
What I am seeing is empty
space opening.
What I am seeing is an
opportunity waiting.
What I am seeing is useless.

What I am seeing is force exerted to
the right and left causes an upward
motion.
What I am seeing is a chair slowly
turning upside down.
What I am seeing is solitude.
What I am seeing is a hollow place.
What I am seeing is space carved.
What I am seeing is floating.
What I am seeing is light.
What I am seeing is caught in a web.

Nikola Tesla
ELECTRO MAGNETIC MOTOR.
No. 381,968

What I am seeing is double spiders
large enough to eat a chair.
What I am seeing is something not
going anywhere.
What I am seeing is the space
around the chair is empty.
What I am seeing is the space
around the chair is shifting.
What I am seeing is the space
between us is shifting.

Figures 7 & 8:
miles & miles
Karen Christopher & Sophie Grodin

Figures 9 & 10:
Control Signal
Karen Christopher & Sophie Grodin

Figure 1:
miles & miles, Karen Christopher and Sophie Grodin
Image: Manu Valarce
At Chisenhale Dance Space, London, 2016

Figures 2 and 3:
So Below, Gerard Bell and Karen Christopher
Images: Manu Valarce
At TwoFold festival, Chisenhale Dance Space, London, 2017

Figures 4 and 5:
Seven Falls, Teresa Brayshaw and Karen Christopher
Images: Warren Orchard
At Experimentica, Cardiff, 2015

Figure 6:
Control Signal, extract from audience leaflet
See below for details
Design: David Caines

Figures 7 and 8:
miles & miles, Karen Christopher and Sophie Grodin
Images: Manu Valarce
At Chisenhale Dance Space, London, 2016

Figures 9 and 10:
Control Signal, Karen Christopher and Sophie Grodin
Images: Warren Orchard
At Experimentica, Cardiff, 2014

Figure 11, opposite:
Seven Falls, Teresa Brayshaw and Karen Christopher
Image: Warren Orchard
At Experimentica, Cardiff, 2015

Control Signal, extract from audience leaflet:
Left panel:
Nikola Tesla, circa 1890, by Napoleon Sarony.
Nikola Tesla signature.
Nikola Tesla in his Colorado Springs laboratory, next to magnifying
transmitter high-voltage generator, 1899.
'Room text' from DeLillo, Don (1985), *White Noise*, Penguin Books: New
York City, p. 306.
Performance texts by Karen Christopher and Sophie Grodin.

Right panel:
Abstract backdrop of twisting smoke; from http://creativity103.com,
licensed under a Creative Commons Attribution 3.0 License.
A still from the Thomas Edison film *Electrocuting an Elephant*, 1903.
Electromagnetic motor, two images; a rotating magnetic field is a
magnetic field that periodically changes direction.
Performance texts by Karen Christopher and Sophie Grodin.
Unless noted otherwise, all licensed under Public domain via
Wikimedia Commons.

Staying With the Tremble

EIRINI KARTSAKI

I tremble when I am cold or scared or on the verge of making a difficult decision. I shiver at the thought of violence or the memory of intense pleasure. My body reacts to fear, excitement and uncertainty. And most times, I understand how I am feeling, *because* I tremble. Trembling creates some sort of uncertainty: it is unclear why my body trembles, what it reacts to. But also, witnessing someone tremble can lead to uncertainty, both for the trembler and the witness – what might have caused this shaking or murmur or quiver? Trembling is involuntary and, thus, difficult to control. It is a reaction of the body to something. And yet, when it ends, the calmness that follows is more distinct than the one that preceded it. With trembling, there is something else that reverberates too, its affect. Shaking, pulsing bodies create an affect that might be contagious. The murmur of the body might make one recoil or come closer. The embodied forces that constitute the tremor of the body can have that effect.

Gilles Deleuze discusses the quiver in relation to Samuel Beckett's work. He considers the quiver itself as an affect. A writer, Deleuze tells us, may substitute 'he said' with 'he stammered' or 'he cried' or 'he stuttered'. The writer has, therefore, the option to *do it* or *say it without doing it* (Deleuze 1998: 107). There is a third option too, which refers to what happens 'when the stuttering no longer affects pre-existing words, but itself introduces the words it affects'. In this case, 'it is the writer who becomes *a stutterer in language*. He [sic] makes the language as such stutter: an affective and intensive language, and no longer an affectation of the one who speaks' (107). Deleuze pushes it even further: it is not only the language that stutters but also the space, atmosphere or context of words 'that brings together within itself the quiver, the murmur, the stutter, the tremolo, or the vibrato, and makes the indicated affect reverberate through the words' (108). In the latter case, the forests and caves and houses also reverberate with affect, alongside the squeaking of feet and the oscillation of the body. 'Language trembles from head to toe', language itself stutters or murmurs, 'as if the words could now discharge their content' (113). Language stutters when it is strained, and thus, it 'reaches the limit that marks its outside' (114). Language itself trembles and movement stutters, not just that who speaks or moves. And with it, affect reverberates.

There is a moment in Karen Christopher and Sophie Grodin's (2012–17) performance *Control Signal* by the company Haranczak/Navarre when both performers start to shake, to vibrate, to move with control from side to side. Grodin and Christopher shake their arms from side to side, moving as if they do not know that they are moving. They both look ahead. Christopher's shoulders are relaxed, arms shaking by her side. Grodin's right arm is stiff, shaking. This feels like a farewell or a tired hand that is waving goodbye. It feels like someone is asleep with one arm still raised. It is a signal in a traffic light or trying to encourage the crabs to escape the fire. It is also perhaps the smell of something rotten and the attempt to create an air current. I watch this with fascination (Lilian Baylis Studio, Sadler's Wells, 2014). I lean in, sitting on the edge of my seat. The bodies in front of me are ordinary bodies in an ordinary situation of constraint; they are doing something, or they seem to be having something done to them, as if some kind of force is being exerted upon them. Something is moving within them, but they make an effort to hold a specific posture. What is happening to these figures is to do with some kind of force that affects their bodies, an invisible force that models the flesh or shakes it, that causes a spasm. Something is rendered visible through the assumed posture of the two bodies on stage. The perpetual shaking acts on my body; it makes it assume a contorted posture. I seem to want something from this scene, yet I do not yet know what that is, and the force of wanting does things to me and my body.

This writing will consider the politics of trembling as a politics of coping with ever-changing, unstable times. Trembling will be approached as a way of considering what it means to stay with and celebrate uncertainty. Trembling here is not associated with weakness, or the figure of the victim or subordinate, but rather fluctuates between weakness and strength to find power in powerlessness. Trembling teaches us to be truly present; it draws us in and asks questions. There are stories that emerge through the ineffability of trembling, the inarticulacy of murmur, and these are stories we are in need of. Staying with the tremble gives rise to new patterns of living, new ways of engaging with instability, as a place from which to depart in order to become who we are. Trembling causes trouble; it points towards something we might not be able to represent or fix in time and space. It draws attention to the stuttering of the earth, the mumbling of uncertainty, the ambiguity of our stumbling. It invites us to stir through things, to sit with uncertainty, to reverberate with affect. I propose staying with the tremble as a gesture towards staying with uncertainty and understanding the potential of not knowing or not being fixed in time and place. I encounter uncertainty here as a choice, rather than a condition imposed on the individual by others or by external circumstances. I am not, thus, referring to types of uncertainty that may have to do with financial instability or professional precarity. Rather, I see uncertainty as a mode of living one's own life without the cultural or social pressures often encountered in certain contexts. I use three instances of trembling: Haranczak/ Navarre's *Control Signal*, Oblivia's *Entertainment Island* and Tom Richards and Tim Spooner's *Cuteness Forensics*. I draw on Deleuze, Steven Connor and Donna Haraway to develop a politics of trembling, a politics of resisting fixity, stability and certainty (as neoliberal, normative values) and to open up a space for the inarticulacy and ineffability of trembling. In this space, uncertainty and instability start to form as new values that encourage openness, renewal and ambiguity.

The title of this chapter borrows Donna Haraway's book title *Staying With the Trouble: Making Kin in the Chthulucene*. In that, Haraway discusses a new relationship to time, to the present moment:

> In urgent times, many of us are tempted to address trouble in terms of making an imagined future safe, of stopping something from happening that looms in the future, of clearing away the present and the past in order to make futures for coming generations. Staying with the trouble does not require such a relationship to times called the future. In fact, staying with the trouble requires learning to be truly present, not as a vanishing pivot between awful or edenic pasts and apocalyptic or salvific futures, but as mortal critters entwined in myriad unfinished configurations of places, times, matters, meanings. (2016: 1)

Staying with the trouble also means taking responsibility for this moment, not expecting that the future will fix things, that technology will fix things. We require new stories that can emerge through staying with the trouble, stories 'of partial recuperation and getting on together', new ways of living and dying, stories that are 'big enough to gather up the complexities and keep the edges open' (Haraway 2016: 101). Staying with the trouble means becoming-with and rendering capable – opening up possibilities for our life, possibilities rooted in the present moment; it means redoing ways of living and dying, making worlds out of worlds of the now. It also means staying with not knowing, not having any ready-made solutions or quick fixes for this world that is unfolding unexpectedly, and with no remorse in front of our eyes.

I am looking at a video extract by the artists Tom Richards and Tim Spooner. I am looking at a dirty floor on top of which lies a creature. This is neither an animal nor a human, or perhaps both at the same time. The figure is slim, its body is covered in pink and it has long legs and no knees at all. Its head is covered with grey fur, and I can barely see two purple ears sticking out. What is particular about this creature is its legs and feet; the feet look like golf bats, stiff and unmoving. But what happens here is beyond stiff and beyond unmoving. The creature is shaking. The slim creature with the fur head and pink body is shaking. In fact, its left leg is shaking back and forth so much so that after a few shakes, the arm also starts moving and after a few more, the other leg starts moving too. One of the arms, with grey hairs sticking out in the place of a hand, seems firmly placed on the ground. This movement is both in and out of place, in and out of synch; it points towards some kind of equilibrium and disequilibrium at the same time. Nothing transcends it and everything transcends it. It matters. It marks time and is stuck in time. It does and undoes itself at the same time. Its undoing is part of its doing, and it keeps doing it. This movement or its circularity seems to be specific to trembling. It has to do with what trembling has to do with. It both destabilizes and reinforces trembling. It is both its means or mechanism *and* result, the process by which it functions *and* goal.

Steven Connor writes about visible forms of trembling: sneezes, orgasms, fits, rages and religious convulsions. He argues that 'we shake and quake and quiver and tremble and flutter and shudder with anger, with fright, with disgust, with horror, with sexual arousal, in religious ecstasy, in conditions of illness and debility, and then just from old age' (Connor 2008). Shaking is an action-sensation, he professes. This action-sensation is caused by something and also causes something, a response; it is contagious; therefore, it needs to be contained. But what would happen if we did not contain trembling? If we allowed the shaking body to run down the streets and fill the shops and parks and landscapes? Shaking 'compels and sustains itself; it is mesmerising because the sympathetic principle is extended inwards as well as outwards. The shaking creature is lost in self-imitation' (2008). In Parkinson's disease, for instance, 'powerlessness has a presence and a power of its own [...] A strength meets a weakness that is not quite weak enough simply to absorb it, to collapse and vanish under the blow' (2008). Tremor, therefore, 'is a border between a weakness and a strength, a tension and a release [...] Shaking makes things strong and weak at once; it makes them strong enough to shake themselves to pieces' (2008).

Another scene: three middle-aged performers from a foreign country (Finland) come onto the stage. They seem to be looking at each other, as if preparing for a cowboy duel. They are doing something subtly, but it is unclear what that is. It is an individual act, but it somehow also brings them together. They seem to be subtly shaking.

> Timo, what are you doing?
> Annika, I am constantly moving.
> You see I'm constantly moving every single part of my body.
> That's exactly what I thought you were doing, Timo.
>   (Oblivia, *Entertainment Island*, 2009)

Subtly moving across the space, the three performers are shaking. They are shaking and also talking. They are trying something out – like a new game, that might end badly, with the ball crushed under someone's wheels. This is an extract from *Entertainment Island*, a trilogy of works by the Finnish performance group Oblivia, performed at Spill Festival of Performance, Ipswich, 2016. The shaking of the bodies of the three performers (Timo Fredriksson, Anna Krzystek and Annika Tudeer), the shaking of the arms, legs, lips and bodies, places a demand. It draws me in; it demands that I am fully present – it demands that I do not attempt to escape what is, to clear away, the present. It asks me to stay with it, stay with the trouble it proposes. This movement is not interested in what precedes and what follows. Trembling reverberates with affect; shaking imitates itself; its powers derive from powerlessness. These figures never collapse; they keep trembling. And we keep trembling with them. Their tremor makes them strong and weak at once. Through the shaking, they discover something new – a new way of becoming-with and rendering possible. The performer shakes, but also the movement stutters. Everything happens in this moment. Someone is drowning; the evacuation of a body; the sinking of the ship. It is a bit like shouting, but silent.

Later on,

> My whole body is in a state of constant motion.
> Now that was interesting.
> Yes, you see, I moved from over there to over here whilst at the same time constantly moving
> every single part of my body.
> I want to try that.
> This opens up a whole new range of possibilities.

Now let me try to sum it up.
We are constantly moving every single part of our bodies
and at the same time moving through
space. Am I right?
    (Oblivia, *Entertainment Island*, 2009)

Trembling is both specific and abstract. It creates an invitation to figure it out, to enter its doing mechanisms, to open up the space of its undoing. Somehow, describing what it does or what we intend to do with it opens up different possibilities. There is an intention that is particular to trembling and to the examples I have chosen to discuss in this writing. There is a particular relationship that trembling opens up, a precise invitation that it extends to us, the audience. Trembling is not working just for itself but for itself and us, or me. We seem to be in this entangled relationship, as if we were a couple. There are multiple couples in this writing: Christopher and Grodin, myself and Spooner, Spooner and Spooner's strange creature, myself and Oblivia. There is also a coupling up of efforts or emotions, the trembling that produces trembling, the stuttering that gives rise to more stuttering, that takes place here.

Christopher and Grodin's shaking is a movement that stutters. A movement that is perhaps unable to speak and stutters instead. But what if what the moment intends to say is simply that stuttering? What if the stuttering of movement *is* its speech? In the latter case, movement becomes an affective and intensive language, a language that stutters; with it, the space, the stage and the surroundings stutter too. Shaking releases something. It makes way for something. It acts both as an incubator, a container of sorts, and a conductor – not a musical conductor but one that transfers currency. Shaking transmits something; it allows the flow of shaking to come through, its frequency or momentum. In other words, shaking *is* what it produces, and it produces what *it is*. Its structure, shape or form is what it puts forward for others to experience, and that structure, shape or form is necessary in order for others to experience what it puts forward. Shaking is both the means and the result – shaking produces shaking, and that is the point. It charges not only the particles it comes in contact with but also its own particles. Its chain of momentum transfer is what shaking achieves. It functions not only like current but also like the conduit that produces current. The two trembling bodies here reproduce themselves as trembling bodies. Trembling's goal, in this case, is to reproduce itself as trembling.

There is something within this shaking, something that reverberates and wants to come out. But what is inside shaking is shaking itself, not some other substance in an icing sugar shaker or a flour sifter. This is a different machine. One that sifts and shakes itself, one that shakes itself to pieces. Deleuze suggests that Beckett's stuttering appears 'as if the words could now discharge their content' (1998: 113). Language's content may have to do with the meaning or sound or even the material of language. But what is the content of shaking in this case? What is the material of trembling?

Another scene later on, from *Cuteness Forensics*, a collaboration again between Tim Spooner and Tom Richards (The Yard Theatre, NOW19, 2019). Spooner, dressed in a strangely tender outfit that leaves his calves exposed and with sponges in the place of shoes, is holding a stick. This is a stick with a hook at its end; the stick is shaking. Spooner extends his arms and tries to reach what looks like a maquette home, which is suspended from the ceiling. The extended stick is shaking; Spooner's calves are shaking; his sponge shoes, though soft and accommodating, are not able to hold his weight. Or maybe not. Maybe the issue here is not his weight at all. Maybe it is simply that any action of any intensity in that particular moment would feel precarious and lonely. Its affect is that of a tremble, a precarious thing that is about to take place. And indeed, there is an action here. It looks intense, so it must be. The action, or else the aim of the scene, is somewhat ambiguous. It is to reveal the interior of the house, by pulling the façade of the house down with a stick, or to break down the house or to destroy the house. Not in its entirety but still. Spooner extends the stick, the stick is trembling, the arm is trembling, the calves are trembling; it is reaching the house, the front door, the windows. The curtains are trembling, the façade made of pink felt is trembling. Is this a real house? Is this my house? I am staying with the tremble, as it carries me away. And I remember this moment now:

I am in the aeroplane; I have visited my dentist in Greece for a procedure. I have also used this opportunity to see Dimitris, who is lovely and calm and accepts me the way I am. And we have decided to end it. This is someone who gave me joy and made no demands of me whatsoever. And yet, there was something about our interaction that felt fastened in its place. But is not that the point after a while? Yes and no. There is an affect, an intensity that feels a little like trembling. That has to do with not knowing, with remaining in and out of place. There is a feeling that has to do with uncertainty that feels a little like trembling.

This uncertainty is full of potential; it tells you that things are not fixed, they can change. It tells you that it is ok for things to change. It tells you that you do not have to remain this way or that way; you do not have to be *any* way. Any *one* way. Anyway. I dreamt of myself in a new city, perhaps New York. I dreamt of myself not knowing. Visiting new places, new streets, new parks, new open-air spaces. I dreamt of myself being that person who visits new places, new streets, new parks, new open-air spaces. In that journey, my body is in a state of constant motion. I move from here to there while trembling. I move every single part of my body. This opens up a whole new range of possibilities. I want to try that. Like a new raincoat or ice-cream flavour. It is an odd taste, a little tight on the shoulders, but it fits: my body is unstable, uncertain, ambiguous and open to this world. Not in any particular way, but in all ways. Relating to one particular person or place or work or institution creates fixity; the necessity of identity or the semblance of that necessity. What I want and perhaps strive for is relating to people, places, work or institutions and their structures without that necessity. Doing this relating while trembling.

The suspended house with the pink felt curtains is trembling. The stick is trembling; my insides are trembling. I am here and there, now and then. I am this kind of person and that. I am not one thing. The house with the pink felt curtains is trembling. Spooner's arm is extended; the hook is trembling. The hook is catching one curtain, opens an opening; like a hook on the fish's mouth, it is trembling, wanting to live, wanting to die. This moment of not knowing, of in-betweenness, of being on the verge of something matters to me. It matters, because the things that seem to make me unhappy are the things that have to do with fixity, certainty, having to be *this* or *that* way. Things that demand that I am or behave like someone who *knows*. I do not want to name things. Because then I have to know. Once I start naming who I am, what I want, what kind of interaction this is or might be, I start fixing things, in their place, in places that do not make sense. I do away with ambiguity and uncertainty and I place pins on the map, on my skin, on the façade of the house; here and here and here. Things cease to tremble.

What I want, in ending things with someone who cares about me, is to keep trembling. I want my house to tremble, its curtains to tremble, its table to tremble. I want to be able to get into my bed at night while it trembles. I want my glasses to be on the verge of the shelf, I want to hear them falling one by one, breaking, smashing on the concrete floor, I want them to tremble. A little like that short story, in which the room becomes smaller and smaller, my house trembles more and more.

And that reveals things, or opens things up, or breaks things. That trembling also brings pleasure. The breaking, the opening up, the renewing, the not knowing. And I am not scared of renewal, of shatter or of breakage. I am used to it. I welcome it. Sometimes, while crying in the airport on the phone to my parents; sometimes, while walking, or dancing, or shaking. Sometimes, while watching. Sometimes, I shake so hard on my seat while watching others tremble that I myself think I have caused a minor earthquake. But it is not an earthquake, it is simply living a life with wonder and curiosity, opening my eyes to things I am unaware of, opening my body up to uncertainty.

I relate to things, places and bodies on and off the stage. In this entanglement, in this dual relationship, I stay with the tremble. I accept and strive for what I am not able to fix or represent. Through trembling, an affective model of being with the other emerges: as an individual, an audience member, a person who shakes when entangled in relation to the other, I join the other and produce more trembling. This stuttering is the means and the goal. It is not fixed and it can change; it does not behave like someone who knows. It explores living and being with the other through wonder and curiosity. It discovers a new way of becoming-with and rendering possible. In this space of inventive connection, of learning to live with one another, I keep trembling. I stay with ambiguity and ambivalence, with what is not yet or will never be. I stay with not knowing without being afraid. I become by staying with the tremble, I embrace the thing I am not, the thing that I might never be. My task is not to be phased by the murmuring bodies, the bodies that become others. It is to stay with the tremble and see where it might take me. My task is to realize the scale of things: the body moves but also the earth trembles. I realize, after all, that the stuttering of the earth becomes one with the stuttering of the movement. My body, in entanglement with the bodies on stage, opens up; it is an ineffable, inarticulate body that stutters. And that stuttering movement *is* its speech that extends inwards and outwards, keeping the edges open.

References

Beckett, Samuel (1967), *Stories and Texts for Nothing*, New York: Grove Press.

Christopher, Karen and Grodin, Sophie (2012–17), *Control Signal*, Haranczak/Navarre Performance Projects, https://karenchristopher.co.uk/project/control-signal/. Accessed 22 December 2020.

Connor, Steven (2008), 'The Shakes: Conditions of Tremor', *The Senses and Society*, 3, pp. 205–20, http://stevenconnor.com/shakes.html. Accessed 25 February 2020.

Deleuze, Gilles (1998), *Essays Critical and Clinical* (trans. D. W. Smith and M. A. Greco), London and New York: Verso.

Haraway, Donna (2016), *Staying With the Trouble: Making Kin in the Chthulucene*, Durham, NC: Duke University Press.

Oblivia (2009), *Entertainment Island*, https://vimeo.com/35881484. Accessed 25 February 2020.

Richards, Tom and Spooner, Tim (2019), *Cuteness Forensics*, The Yard Theatre, London, NOW19, private link.

What Never Stops?

JOE KELLEHER

The following conversation with Karen Christopher and Sophie Grodin took place on the stage of the Chelsea Theatre on 10 October 2013, after the first London performance of *Control Signal*. The conversation was led and 'loosely edited' by Joe Kelleher.

Joe: There are various moments early in the show when you are both stood in those two doorways at the back of the stage. And you're really still. I'm reminded of those clocks you see in old European squares, which have these wooden figures that come out according to a certain schedule, and they perform an action. They don't know when the action is going to happen because they are just made of wood, so they are simply going to do this thing, on the hour or whenever it might be. But of course you are not made of wood. In fact, you are actual people. And so, there is something else in these early moments of the show, a dynamic, which has to do with the fact that you've rehearsed what you are doing. It's obvious you have rehearsed it. In fact, you are telling us that you have rehearsed it. You're effectively saying to us: This has been tried out before, and if we do what we are doing in this way, there should be a particular effect. But then again … not necessarily. Because we haven't tried this out here, for real. It may be something else will happen, something wonderful which will be quite other than the expected effect. The business has been rehearsed and prepared, yes, but at the same time, 'What if …?'

Karen: I like that a lot. One of the things we started with, and I think some of what you're saying comes from this, is the idea of invisible influences. So you may think that you are operating with this or that understanding in mind or that you are being affected in a particular way, but you have to be open to the fact that it's not in black and white and you could get it wrong. You can get it very wrong. In fact, you can be very certain for a long time and then you realize you're in the wrong part of the polar icecap, or wherever. And all of a sudden, it's very serious. And I think part of that getting lost and the question of did you mean to get lost or not get lost, the work is connecting into that too.

Sophie: There is repetition but there are also these breaks in it all the time. It's something that maybe only became clear in the later part of the process, as things were supposed to be finished. But there's a vibration. There are certain moments that will never be finished because for whatever reason, these moments were kept shaky, kept vibrating. No matter what, there will always be this uncertainty, and in the end, we just allow it to be.

Joe: Hence the enigma of the title of the work. *Control Signal.* The beam that controls us, or the signal that is used to control how things happen. Although of course things don't necessarily allow themselves to be controlled. Something I enjoyed particularly about the structure of the show is that it 'goes somewhere'. There is the sense that at the end, we are somewhere else from when we started out. But also there is the possibility that it can go somewhere else at any particular moment. There is, for example, an effect of silence that comes at certain moments. Or the darkness falls, actually and metaphorically. Or we might be enjoying a particular sequence, but then the work goes in another direction. One of the places it goes to is history, and it goes to a sympathy with people from history. Something happened: the Rosenbergs were executed in America in the mid-twentieth century, convicted of spying for the Soviet Union. At the beginning, I don't have that as something to deal with, but it has leaked through what you are doing on stage, and so now, I'm reading that chair as the electric chair, and I am reading the shudders you make in the same way, not exclusively as 'this is what that means' but it becomes part of how I see it. So for me there's a really powerful accumulation of effects which has to do with something behind the performance. A story even. There is a story, or there is the sense of a story that might have been told, there's a sympathy with regard to things that happened in the world and which are being re-ghosted here. And for me that becomes a movement of the show, and part of its power.

Karen: Sophie and I wandered in the darkness together and tried to figure out what would happen. And we made a set of plans, we set out an avenue of investigation. But instead of saying 'We're going there', we said 'Let's walk like this and see where we end up'. And so I think the Rosenbergs were a surprise to us, but they were an obvious surprise. When we found them, we said, 'Oh right, everything we are doing leads to this'. And then there was Edward Snowden and other things that said, 'pick me' in a very serious way. Electricity was there the whole time, and if you start looking into electricity …

Sophie: Topsy had been there from the beginning. One of the very first things we ever did was the Topsy leg, the quivering leg. And thinking back now, Topsy led to Ethel Rosenberg, led to the idea of electrocution, or electricity being used as a means to go through a body and to control the body.

Karen: Topsy was an elephant who was killed at the suggestion of Thomas Edison. She was killed with electricity because he wanted to discredit alternating current, which Nikola Tesla and Westinghouse, the American company, had the patent on, and Edison had the patent on direct current. So he wanted everyone to think alternating current is really dangerous. So here is an elephant and we want to put this elephant to death. Let's do it in public and do it with electricity because elephants are huge and invincible and if it can kill an elephant, it's 'bad' and everyone will be afraid of it. There's a YouTube clip you can still see, since Thomas Edison was also doing early films, he filmed it, so you can see an electrocution of an elephant, which is Topsy. And the first thing I said to myself is, well, you certainly can't equate Ethel and the elephant. And then of course if you can't do it … you …

Joe: … you do it.

Karen: Which is not to say they are equated of course. But they are used together, in a way. And they're both female.

Joe: That uncertainty as to whether you can do this – and then there they are, doing it – one way of thinking about that is around how we the audience read the two of you: what kind of figures or creatures you are. You're both wearing a sort of housecoat uniform on stage. At a certain point, you are tent-show entertainers, as in ladies and gentlemen, there is an elephant, roll up roll up. As in it's educational, sure, but give us your money. And then at another point you are operators of the machine, whatever the hell the machine is. Or experimenters. And those roles, when they are happening, they are quite defined, but they can also easily slip into something else. It is not a mish-mash, there is a rhetoric to each of those particular roles. But then that starts producing, for me, an interesting uncertainty as to what it is these two performers might or might not be showing us, or demonstrating, or what sort of knowledge is at stake here.

Sophie: This idea of the changes between the different modes that you're talking about is something we worked with a lot. Different modes of how we are communicating, how we are telling something, how we are performing. There was sometimes a very fluid transition into something that then very slowly merges into something else. At other times, it is important that those changes are very, very sudden, because then it jumps into a different time and a different mode and a different feeling. I think those transition modes are also there when there is an allowance for small mistakes, or when we are showing that we are now ready to go into this, or we are showing that we have now left that behind and that we can move into the next thing.

Joe: One of the reasons those moments register for me is something to do with rhythm. It's partly to do with what the two of you are doing on stage. Certain effects of rhythm are established, which you can then afford to break, although often quite delicately. This has to do with how an audience might relate to the piece physically and mentally. The sound, the music, which Boris Hauf has designed, is fantastic. It makes me think of weather systems for instance, but then there is the sound of a hand clapping, or of a chair being scraped. And then there are the silences around that, which again start producing these rhythmic blocks, where those little swerves and diversions can be registered as events.

Karen: One of things we did was we decided to make little field trips for ourselves. In this situation, the thing about composing a performance directive is that it controls the work. So if you have one person who makes all of those instigations or whatever, that person pulls the strings. And that's fine, if you like that. But in our collaboration, it was important that we each had control over how to pull the strings. So we each had different ways of coming up with 'We'll do this a little bit and we'll do that a little bit and see what happens'. I think what I can say from my point of view, from the kinds of things that I like to do, is I like to put us in action. It might mean going on a little field trip to somewhere and having to do something or observe something and then figure out how to pull something performative out of that, to do for each other or with each other. Or if it's in the studio, where you are not going out into the world, it might mean coming up with a task that has to be performed and then performing it and seeing what happens. Now that task might be something very simple like finding a performative answer to the question 'What never stops?' So if we both have to answer 'What never stops?' we go off into separate corners and we think about it for a little bit and then we direct each other, or we try to do a thing that occurred to us in answer to the question 'What never stops' But it doesn't answer the question in words necessarily. It is something that you perform.

Sophie: It was important that we didn't always perform our own directives. You swap. And having someone else's directive that has been shaped around an idea that you have shared before makes you do something that you would never come up with yourself. And then to look at each other and to have that other person's eyes while you do something that is happening in that moment, suddenly there is something there. So I think the swapping and the observing each other and then working from that was very important.

A member of the audience: Can you actually pass words through the air between you?

[*This question refers to a faux Victorian-era mind-reading act that occurs in the performance.*]

Sophie: [*deadpan*] In the end, we managed to do it.

Karen: [*not so deadpan*] We did it! You saw us do it!

Audience member: But seriously.

Karen: I think so, after a while. We believe.

Joe: You say that. You say 'You saw us do it'. But one of the things I was noticing, for example in the chair duet sequence, where you make the chair rise in the air between you, is that you don't watch what you are doing. You get us to watch it. So the chair rises up, but you've both got your backs to it. You are focused on your task: if we do this, it will make this other thing happen for them, the audience. But you don't see yourselves do it, we do.

Karen: It's true. Sophie and I miss most of the show. Sometimes I have no idea what she is doing.

Another member of the audience: One of the things that never stops is a performative relationship to capital punishment, for example. And I don't know enough about the Rosenbergs but I know a bit about Topsy and the sense that it was a tussle between these two people who had different models of electricity and so on. But also that Topsy had been sentenced to death for the crime of trampling her keeper –

Karen: – who was awful to her –

Audience member: Indeed. But anyway there was a functionality to it as there was with the Rosenbergs. Is that a vibration that relates to the thing that Joe just pointed out, some kind of associative connection, that you show us these things that happen, like the chair rising, in a way that associates to what you are doing? Another performative showing?

Karen: Yes, it's like 'If this and this and this ... then what do you think? What do you make of that?' I think it's really easy to look back, if you were to do so, at the Rosenbergs, and to say 'See how wrong it is?' But I think with things that are happening right now, for a lot of people, it's hard for them to say how they feel about a thing that's happening in world politics because you think 'Well, I don't know everything'. Or people say 'I'm not sure about ...' Of course there are some people who are always sure about everything. But there's quite a few people, I think, who aren't so sure, and that's resonating with this too, I hope. It's that tension between looking at something and agreeing that it is what you think it is. Or looking out of the corner of your eye at it and thinking 'But I don't have to look at it and I don't have to deal with it'. You know what I mean? It feels to me like there is something about that in the piece.

Invisible Partners Remain Themselves Inside
Thick Descriptions of Migrating Gestures

LITÓ WALKEY

The following micro-vignettes of writing look into a series of choreographic projects that have unfolded over the past twenty-five years. They can be read as 'thick descriptions' in the sense that they are calling out to the multiple voices, temporalities and parameters that exist as co-equal, mutually independent and fully collaborative partners inside the processes. Rather than merging tracelessly into the service of a representative terminus, these partners 'remain themselves inside'. Particular and transforming, each partnership is an encounter, an intersection, a portal, a source of energy and a point of departure.[1] Suspended in a force of reoccurrence, the details of these invisible partners appear to us in such a way as to make a turn in our mind, to reach somewhere, open something and make some gesture.[2]

Standing next to each other – Squint
From twenty-five years ago

A colleague choreographed a duet for a guy called Dean and myself. The duet was a story with our hands. Our hands landing on points of our torso and out to points in the space. Carving lines and telling some kind of unheard story. We stood side by side and walked forward together. We stopped and slowly moved through the sequence. Our lower bodies were rooted, and our torsos carried lines with our hands and arms. We followed the lines in unison, not looking at each other with our eyes but staying in synch

1. Inspired by Lyn Hejinian's articulations in *Positions of the Sun*, 'Each element of the work, every particular, exists as a point of encounter, rather than of separability; each particular serves as an intersection, a portal, a source of energy, and a point of departure (rather than a terminus). The semantic temporality (which I'm inclined to term the paratactic present) of paratactic attention is closely akin to Gertrude Stein's "beginning again and again": we come to one thing and another in a moment to moment place to place sequence and series of experiences experienced without any necessary or determined order. Their details appearing in such a way as to make one conscious of them and to assure that they "never", as Adorno puts it, "merge tracelessly into the totality"'. Lyn Hejinian (2018), *Positions of the Sun*, New York: Belladonna* Collaborative, p. 21.

2. Drawing from Renee Gladman's *Calamities* in which she writes 'Someone raised her hand. I don't remember who. She said, "We might not like your questions," but said it while smiling with her arm still up. I had to go on with my lecture: "When you turn in your mind, you reach somewhere, open something, make a gesture". I paused. My notes had quotes around them. I was almost done'. Renee Gladman (2016), *Calamities*, Seattle/New York: Wave Books, pp. 3–4.

through our bodies. We would start a gesture together and have it land together at the same time. We did this in rehearsal, in a studio. We did this in performance, for friends and for the Vancouver dance community. In a workshop some time later, I was asked to perform something and decided to do this duet on my own. I negotiated with Dean although he was not there. The connection became visible, a few people who had seen the duet with Dean said they could still see him. A year later, I was invited to perform a solo for admission into a choreography school in Amsterdam. I had not taken time to prepare anything new. Quite spontaneously, I decided to perform this duet again. I entered while talking inaudibly to Dean. Turning my head in his direction to make reference to his presence, I went through the slow phrase of our gestures. I performed with the one who is not there or who is there but not visible.

I am remembering the precisely crafted material that makes up a physical sequence. Through the air, my gestures are resting on Dean's pathways. That 'resting' shapes the movement. Even when Dean's movement is not visible, it is there in my movement. I am entering from the back side of the studio, curving a path forward towards the audience. Stepping with slight hesitation, all my movements tilt slightly to the side, aligning with my partner.

A dance for one is made between two – wings raised to a second power[3]
From eighteen years ago

Two of us meet once in the studio for about three hours: I will do some dancing, whatever comes, while you watch. Then you do the same from what you saw. You do more of what you saw, while I watch. Then I will do something again, repeating the focus I have seen in you. But we are not talking or negotiating in between. Just dancing one after the other. A relay that goes on for a bit. Then we talk. Briefly. We acknowledge a certain thing has come to be. This is the dance we have made together. We name the parts that we perceive. We map it out and give the whole dance a name. Then I perform it again. We might make some adjustments to refine it and bring the form or intention closer to what we had been noticing.

---

3. This title comes from Simone Weil's *Gravity and Grace*, translated by Arthur Wills. 'To come down by a movement in which gravity plays no part [...] Gravity makes things come down, wings make them rise: what wings raised to a second power can make things come down without weight? Creation is composed of the descending movement of gravity, the ascending movement of grace and the descending movement of the second degree of grace'. Simone Weil (1997), *Gravity and Grace* (trans. A. Wills), Lincoln: University of Nebraska Press, Bison Books, p. 48.

I repeat this process with other people. Always the same kind of relay between two of us, leading to an agreed upon solo. Then I practice this series of solos on my own. To re-engage with each dance, I connect my thoughts to the person I made it with, with the situation of our brief meeting and to all the details we agreed on. Rather than trying to improve or develop the solo, my effort is to re-align with the material and the circumstance of its creation. Attempting to attend to a string of ready-mades.

Some years ago, she was thinking about 'an occasion for unselfing' – something she read from Iris Murdoch. This eventually led her to think about creating a solo as a site of beauty separate from the self. She gathered a list of 'how-tos' like 'how to double consciousness by losing it in a certain way'; 'how to set up, reveal or answer an expectation beyond verbal expression'; 'how to shift receptiveness of matter'; and 'how to train imitative, empty repetition and mimetic obedience'.

She wanted to create something to practice and she wanted to create this through dialogue. So she invited eight choreographers to meet with her for a few hours in the studio, one at a time, to make a short dance. In each meeting, they alternated dancing for each other. They responded physically and came to an agreement about what the solo dance had become. In each meeting, a dance for one was made between two. Eight meetings took place. She has eight dances to practice. She keeps them each as similar as possible to what they became during their meeting of creation. She practices these dances in sets of three, in random order. In performance, she does three sets, beginning each set with the dealing of cards, to determine which dance and which order.

Portraits of one and another – Where's the rest of me?
From seven years ago

I led a group of choreography students through some generative processes. Language, movement and collective memories gathered through pathways of reiteration and reformulation. Working with a selection of their material, students created three-minute performative responses to a written directive. As a composite of colliding suggestions, the directive I gave them was an invitation to 'reach visibility' through registers of self-portraiture, constraint and exposure and to 'make a middle' by concealing or removing something. The students' three-minute solos were packed with specific articulations, oscillating between different forms of address and performativity. They each made a script that mapped what was said and done as a referential artefact that could support the performance to happen again.

During an artistic research seminar of my own, I shared five of the three-minute performances from my students. To keep each one discrete, I resisted any reinterpretation or combining. The memory of each performance was close, and I had the scripts. I moved myself into physical positions, temporary set-ups, that charged the alignment of my memories to each student as I had seen them in their performance. The discrepancy between my memory, the script and the fact that I am not them was a vibrating area of play. This developed into a solo called 'Where's the rest of me?' Through the accumulating layers of re-iterations, my effort was to keep calling back the initial performances. To meet again in memory and through script that other person who made this and did that. I was not the first time. I was not only me.

The first time, Céline had positioned herself behind a small podium that happened to be in the studio. She read three sections from her notebook, as her upper body leaned slightly over a microphone. In the first section, her words came as a list of indexical sentences, with numbers or extra words added at the end of each one. They came in lists and we went many places. With those words, we changed our age and remembered what can happen. 'Nine months, a dream, a pinch, a jump and a chair'. Facts were stated and then they blew away. Next was a section of announcements. A list of what this, these words, could be. 'A song to sing, a song to see, a song to draw, a song to continue, a song to tell, a song to write each day'. And then at the end were suggestions of what could be done, if necessary. 'Stand on a chair, stay back, speak in a microphone, don't speak at all'.

After Céline, there were all the times that followed. I had her words in my notebook; a microphone on a stand with a long cable running behind it moved over to a chair; a wooden drafting board stood on its side between the chair and the microphone stand. I stood on the chair, leaned over the board and adjusted the microphone stand to a folded angle. This physical set-up aligned me with my memory of Céline. She had stood at a certain distance away from us and leaned over the podium, exposing her half-bodied portrait. I stood too high, leaning over uncomfortably to reach my mouth in the direction of the microphone. While stabilizing the board that concealed the chair I was standing on and the lower part of my body, I held up a notebook to read her words.

The first time, Neils had told us what he was going to do before he did it, said what he was going to say after he said it, projected us forward and asserted us back. He made a general announcement: 'Please don't time this performance because the timing makes part of it'. Pointing at someone, he asked one of the audience members to start a stop watch. 'Can you please stop watch three minutes? Can you take the time please? We already started, so start at two minutes'.

After Neils, there were all the times that followed. I had his script on my phone and fumbled to read it from my screen. It told me what to do and what to say about what I had already done. Everything was set up for me to set up what was already set up and I addressed the audience, who were sitting around a table, and asked if someone could take the time. 'Say everything you do. So when you begin, say for example, "I begin" and then you start. Make a clear beginning. Say: "So hello, my name is Johnny or Charley, the next performance you will see is about self-portraiture. For that you need to organize a table with the audience sitting around it, and install a microphone." Without introducing or speaking you search for a song with the word "apple" in it. Go through your memory while singing. Don't speak. When you have found the song, ask: "You know what I mean?" Then speak to the audience in a very casual way. Say everything you do. So if you are searching the song, also say that you are searching the song'.

More self than oneself – aswebegin
From seven and three years ago

My works with the dance company in Stockholm continued with what had developed in 'Where's the rest of me?' Similar processes of reformulating and redirecting tangents of development formed episodes of gesture and language. Each dancer combined and juxtaposed these materials to make short compositions that were then performed to a single partner.

During the rehearsal process, partners of two performed for each other. They taught, echoed and amplified back to each other. Every instance of 'doing for the other', 'doing for your partner', 'doing in the presence of your partner' was a mini-performance that included the attentiveness of both sides of the partnership. The prepared composition grew to appropriate all the circumstances that took place in the partners' shared micro-arena of performing and audiencing. The second or third iterations of compositions did not end at the initially prepared form but extended to include the physical and attentive situation of the partner-performance. The particular quality and location of the partner's presence folded into the blueprint memory of the material.

Here again a repeatable unit was formed; the performance maintained a relation to the sources that came together to make its composition, companioned by the situations of having performed it for a partner. The language, timing, placement and gestures were contingent to the situations of having been exposed to another person. The attention, tension and intentions of the audiencing partner carried on in its composition.

When she performs that gesture of lifting the side of the blanket as if to show something, while saying 'Here, this here [...] that', she does this in resonance with the attentions that were already witness to it. She is not alone. She crouches on the floor next to the blanket. She wants to indicate the edges of this temporary territory. She utters a few half-sentences, her body makes some half-indicating gestures. Lifting, folding. Her attention is hovering. Doubling between a 'here of now' and a 'here of then'. The 'now' connects with the space shared by others, to show something, to show them, to be with them in seeing something. And the 'then' connects with an inner communication, with a quality of moment that took place in the past when she first went through these gestures in a private performance with her partner. She is blurring her aloneness. Her aloneness is blurring. The quality of her presence is split and amplified, while the intention, the direction, 'the desire behind' is not clearly underlined or, at least, is not single.

Echoes make a new partner – A round shadow with three points
From three years ago

Three performers created a series of assembled events. Each event combined an indication of the generative premise for an activity, an extract of the material from the activity and a form of praising the material. The demonstrative, the scripted, the performed, the danced, the followed and the listened to assembled together. In this entanglement, the shape of words and the thing and the person appear to come closer.

When all parts of the event became familiar to the performers, it was performed as an 'extreme echo'. Rather than developing a single story, the performers assembled a communication of reoccurring fragments from different aspects of the material. By recalling, redoing and retelling, they accessed traces from memory and the present moment. The performers conversed musically with overlap and relay. What had already been perceived between three people doubled and emerged as a new partner – a 'scribble' of echoes.

This is a collective vision. Identically remembering another person's variation and building a kind of architecture around it. This is not a story but a dance that moves language into the middle. This is co-composition, suspended in the force of a reoccurrence.

I invited partners to look with me at particular details in our direct environment. Rather than falling on recognizable, identifiable subjects, our visions framed temporary assemblages of details. The activity was to point out and give words to what was happening at the intersection of commonly overlooked entities, partial and consequential, such as the meeting between a shadow, a trace of dirt and a hole in a surface. The imaginative space between a piece of language and a junction of details in the environment was treated as a strange object that opened a distinct process of observation.

She brought her over to the same place. 'Step away a little bit from the wall, so there's a space between, and if you turn', she said, 'if you turn and look over there, you see two [...] dots. And each eye can rest on a dot, one dot is next to the other dot. They are actually holes in the surface but they don't go in very deep so they are more like dots and if you keep your eyes resting on the two dots, you can see just above is a white smudge (the heel of a hand gestures upward in the air as if to be making the smudge), and if you keep looking, it's like a cloud that is floating above the dots'.

Afterwards, on my own, I practiced intervals of 'refrain': to the situation when my partner asked me to come over to a certain location to see something and to when I asked my partner to come over to another location to see something else; to the names we gave or to our effort to reach the words that best aligned with the nameless entities; to the visual memory of the indicated detail, which triggered more memory of the words; to the positions we moved to – crouching, leaning, lying, standing – to optimally access the visual of the detail and to the light that shifted while what was in front of our eyes transformed through the excessive attention we gave it.

I was referring to the details that were not visible anymore, but they were still there. These details called on a web of words that descriptively and associatively referred to an observation that had taken place in the past.

There had been a brief moment of shared concentration between two people. One person had looked, spoken and indicated, while the other had looked and listened. These small moments, gathered around small areas of perception, connected to gestures and physical locations. They impressed themselves into strings of spoken words. There is a space between two people being attentive together, present but not visible. And a partner by my side, present but not visible.

To work on a choreographic project together, six of us first met each other in duet encounters over a period of a few months. Leading and following each other for a day, we engaged in different modes of exchange and curiosity. We met at the cemetery during the last days of summer; on the train speeding away from Berlin towards another German city; in the studio with a piece of poetry between our bodies and a tiled wall; on a boat motoring across the dark waters through the moonlit night; at the exhibition of an artist who we did not actually come to see.

After all the meetings took place, we came together as a group of six, wondering what was relevant to bring into the common round from the individual meetings and how to share what had happened. We composed artefacts to recover, reinvent and exchange fragments of memory. Make-shift installations and storytelling eventually settled into small pieces of language. Formed by two perspectives, each encounter was recalled through these pieces of language.

Before visiting the exhibition, they got to know each other while sitting in an outdoor cafe, buying lunch and sitting on some grass in a public square. They retrospected into their own years of working in the fields of dance. Their constellations crossed over at certain points and people. They reflected on the time in their work lives when they were wanting much more than what they knew they wanted. In the exhibition, the storytelling was immediate and direct and sometimes literally backed us up against the wall. For talking so long they were too familiar, they were too familiar for talking so long. And there was no room for us to listen.

A roll of dice before each performance determined which three encounters we would re-tell. For the duration of an hour, the six of us moved through the selected encounters, giving an extended focus to one and then the other, and eventually accumulating and mixing all three. We began and finished each others' sentences, we repeated single words, we allowed gaps of silence and we spoke in unison. We made an effort not to forget the details and to listen for new ones. We dug into the words and we dug into the listening. Our words sparked associated bits of images, bits of sound and bits of other words. As six people, we constructed a polyphony that honoured 'thinking around' the inchoate memories observed between two people.

Next time it will have been with other people –
The Circulating Book Project
From three years ago and today

I am adding some imprints into the pages of a blank notebook: colour, line, language, thread and paper. They land on the page in correspondence with the co-authors of the book. We are three companion authors who circulate the book between us through a collectively devised structure. This long-term artistic exchange takes the form of a book as a site of experimentation. Distinct content and materiality emerge through collage, drawing and erasure techniques, as well as modes of language, correspondence and collaboration. Through this process, we engage in acts of response, anticipating the 'other' and connectively associating with the emergent pages in the book.

The multiple unfoldings of this collaboration set up a distribution of forces that operate beyond the notion of the subject, emphasizing the intersubjective and transindividual. The book is not only a book but a series of intricate and intimate processes that inform, pass through and index what is in and out of the book.

On the last pages she has spent time with, something is happening. A question from a few pages before is repeated with faint pencil in the upper left corner. 'What pours in?' And a field of gold covers the bottom half of the page. The opposite page has a spread of punctured holes. Holes the size of a needle. Paper has been pushed out at the openings, forming ridges around the holes. When she looks at it from the side, holding the page horizontally in front of her eyes, it looks like sand has fallen onto the surface.

Alongside our entries into the book is a circuitous process of passing the book between the three of us. Individual 'messengers' are invited to deliver the book. These specifically designed deliveries wedge unexpected, intimate and transient exchanges into our daily rhythms. The traces of these encounters travel along and potentially make their way into the book. As I work on my pages, I think about who the next person to deliver the book could be, possibly a friend who the next author has not met before, and I arrange where in the city the delivery meeting could take place. I record a message for them on a cassette tape that travels with the book. They will listen to the message together and follow what it suggests they do for their brief encounter. The recording is composed through a combination of the suggestions I followed when the book was last delivered to me, an aspect of something happening in the pages of the book and my anticipation of these two people's first meeting.

'Hello, thanks for managing to meet. Here's a little suggestion for something I'd like you to do together. It won't take much time, but there are a few parts to it. You might like to listen through all the suggestions first and then go back and listen to each part again. As you sit side by side, turn to look at the shadows in each other's face. Each choose one shadow that you see and take turns describing it to your partner in a few sentences. Then look around at the shadows near the bench where you're sitting. It's probably already getting dark at the time of your meeting so you could look for shadows made from the street lights. Each choose a shadow that you see and take turns describing it to your partner. Choose one of the descriptions you told your partner (either the face shadow or place shadow) and take turns re-telling your description. Focus on saying what you said, instead of editing or saying what you see now, and include a small part (a sliver) from one of your partner's descriptions into what you're re-telling. Next to the book there are some extra sheets of paper and a pen. Please write down each other's last description and leave them to keep traveling with the book'.

———————————————

Were you building the present? The shadows said so.[4]

Collective processes of generating with others join an inquiry into articulations of personhood, authorship, ownership, agency, transindividuation and production that resist a totality of representative composition or development driven by personal intention. Instead of processes that begin and end with 'I' and engage collaborators for the purpose of single-authored goals, collective processes nurture a proliferating potential in the generative space among memory, presence and collective thinking.

Invisible partners remain themselves inside. In doing so, they enable choreography to emerge as a lateral figure, an afterthought or as the unseen but felt organizing pattern within creative processes; they activate elemental events to be experienced as parts that can be arranged and rearranged indefinitely and they bring perception to what has happened or what lies in the interstices of the undone, or to edges of recognitions outside of yourself.

4. Borrowing again from a string of Renee Gladman's words in *Calamities*, where she writes, 'Were you building the present? The shadows said so'. Renee Gladman (2016), *Calamities*, Seattle/New York: Wave Books, pp. 45–46.

The Promise of More to Come (So Below)

MARY PATERSON

Steam rises from the teapot at the back of the stage. At some point – if not now, then surely later – the water will be poured, and steam will rise from the cup. That's what freshly boiled water is – anticipation, preparation. The promise of more to come.

So Below is a duet that unfolds as if Karen Christopher and Gerard Bell know what's going to happen, but they haven't discovered it yet. It appears like a story glimpsed in a stream of words that have tumbled out of a book in the wrong order. To watch, it is surprising. To remember, it is full of sensory pleasure, like a mist of steam rising from a silver spout.

Sometimes, you can hear Karen's footsteps before you see her: the sound is a crunch of boots on something hard, and it sounds of longing. You think: *if only I could dance a ritual like Karen and Gerard and make absent bodies reappear. If only I could make the sound of Karen into something corporeal.* They dance like they're praying – swinging back and forth with the words of gravestone inscriptions falling from their lips, their tidy bodies folding and unfolding like envelopes of magic.

But that comes later.

First, they dance like they're dancing. They slip into a stageshow routine – something nostalgic. The song is a crackly recording of unrequited love, and the stage is ripe with things that are missing. Their bodies move gently together in rhythm, except when they do not. You look closer, and think: *This is not harmony. This is something more veiled and modest, like a shy sister hiding her face from my gaze.*

Sometimes, you can sense things before you see them. Here are mounds of earth waiting for future roots and here is water, steaming with anticipation. Here are four feet kicking out in music hall style. Here are the elements – comforting and soft – of our mortal earth.

She hovers, she teeters ... she almost falls. (But that was earlier.)

Sometimes, you don't know what is coming. Here are mounds of earth, and here is a foot kicking them into a dusty mess. Here are two hands worrying the dusty mess into flat squares like freshly dug graves. Here is a story about a man who had something to prepare. Here are words coming out of Karen's mouth as if they are as new to her as they are to you.

Steam rises from the teapot.

Gerard has a clutch of pebbles, lost or found. They clatter onto a hard surface, but Karen and Gerard don't turn to listen. Sometimes, they know what each other is doing. Sometimes, one of them leads and the other follows. They work together but apart in quiet disharmony, like a family of veiled sisters. Like the elements: earth and water. Like busy feet, worried hands, the sounds of longing.

And now, they dance like they're praying. They pray for the long dead, the buried, the underground. They pray for the bodies marked in stone as someone's beloved, devoted, dearly missed. The bodies marked by two dates that mean nothing to the living: the day you're born, which you cannot remember, and the day you die, when there is no memory left. The dates fall from Karen's and Gerard's lips like prayers, and the prayers fall from their bodies like veils of magic.

Everything that happened to the beloved happened in the absence in the middle. It happens still, in the sounds off stage – in the questions left unanswered and unsaid.

How does it feel for a grown woman to walk on flowerpots, lifting each pot gingerly as she topples on one leg? What do you hope for when you watch her lose her balance and almost touch a toe to the ground? What is lost when she hops off, picks up her flowerpots and leaves? Can you guess what will happen? Can you guess whose words she borrows when she starts to speak? Whose gestures he copies when he starts to dance? Whose body is itching? When they talk of itches, do they mean the interminable kind or the pleasant kind? Is there a pleasure in watching someone else's discomfort – existential or otherwise? Can you tell there will be an end? Can you tell from the steam rising and the earth arranged in rootless mounds and the chains waiting for buckets and the two people dressed simply like peasants that the stage will vibrate with absent meaning? That in a number of minutes or hours you will be putting your hands together to make a noise? That you will try to work a ritual, form a prayer, to bring their bodies back?

Gerard is an absent body in the middle; but that comes later. Karen would like to jump and remain in the air, like a ghost or a photograph of a breathless moment. Earlier, she nearly fell from a flowerpot tower.

There are three doors in the theatre, and they are all open. Offstage, there are sounds and lights and sometimes movement. Something is happening in the leaks that slide in from elsewhere: it could be a rehearsal, or the main event, or both. It could be two people hovering in mid absence. It could be two people dancing in the middle.

Later, when they dance again, their dances will remember things that have happened recently. A gesture, a glance, a breathless moment. Their bodies hold memories more vivid than a scratch of a date carved into stone.

You think: *No doubt there is steam rising from the teapot, although I have stopped looking. No doubt there is unrequited love, itching, and a shy sister behind every promise of harmony.*

Here is a man, and here is his voice, further away. It is Gerard, and he can imitate the dying. Here is a depiction of what it looks like to communicate with people who are neither present nor absent. This is what happens when a body is as frail as a ghost, with a voice that leaks from the far side of elsewhere.

Earlier, they stood together in silence. When they started to speak, they spoke as if the conversation had already begun.

No doubt there are already people speaking, silently or otherwise, about itching, dying and being born. No doubt there are words under veils and bodies turned to ghosts and sensory pleasures that I had forgotten to remember until they were drawn into this room with a ritual and a dance.

Here is a letter, written some time ago, that outlines the rules of happiness. The letter is being spoken and the speaker is being covered in earth. Here is the silhouette of an absent man, Gerard, who gets up, shakes himself down and stands next to his inverse silhouette. It looks like a man has been killed, marked and buried. You think: *everything that was said about happiness happened in the absence in the middle.*

What do you hope for?

Here is earth and here is water – a drawer full of water, hiding in plain sight, that has been persuaded all of a sudden to make a wave. Here is a flowerpot of water, spilling over Gerard's coiled hand like a spring of life that can't be contained. Here is the middle of something, the sprawling excess of living in all its wasteful necessity.

Here is everything.

Sometimes, you find out just as something happens that you had known about it all along. Karen raises two buckets of water on chains, and water begins to flood the stage like anticipation. Water dripping. Water spilling. Water rushing round the thirsty roots of plants newly tucked into freshly dug graves.

Steam rises from the teapot at the back of the stage. At some point – if not now, then surely later – the water will be poured, and steam will rise from the cup. That's what freshly boiled water is – anticipation, preparation. The promise of more to come.

Here is earth and here is water. Here is fire: candles floating on a drawer of water that sways with the memory of persuasion.

Here are gestures unravelled as if they brim with meaning, but they don't know it yet.

Here is *So Below*. It appears like a truth traced across a pair of bodies that dance a duet almost out of time. To watch, it is surprising. To remember, it is full of sensory longing, like a mist of steam rising from a silver spout.

If only I could touch that water and feel the movement sweep along my fleshy body. I would play it over, like a ritual, or a dance, or a conversation that has already begun.

The stage is empty apart from the elements: earth, water, fire, burial, rebirth, memories, a spillage, the voice of a dying man, the dates of the beloved, the rules of happiness, the sound of unrequited love and a leak of light from elsewhere. The promise of more to come.

You think: *Longing is the sister of anticipation.*

You think: *Karen and Gerard have left the stage with everything in it.*

If only we could turn the knowledge of their absence into something corporeal. We start to clap. We clap a ritual. We clap to bring their bodies back.

We keep clapping.

Mary Paterson saw *So Below* on 20 October 2012,
at Chelsea Theatre, London.

On Creating a Climate of Attention: The Composition of Our Work

KAREN CHRISTOPHER AND SOPHIE GRODIN

Karen and Sophie gathering together

We are two performance makers working together to pull something out of the air around us, out of the cloud of information we become aware of in the context of our gathering together, day after day, month after month, cultivating a piece of performance work between us.

Sophie is a young Danish performance maker who has recently completed a course in performance arts in London. With other local performing artists, she has worked to create a number of performance experiences including *ROOM* (2012), a performance that co-authors a story with one audience member at a time. She is interested in the dialogue that exists between people and space and the arrangement of public space to influence interactions between people.

Karen is a middle-aged American performance maker and teacher. She relocated to London after her Chicago-based performance group Goat Island disbanded in 2009.[1] Her company, Haranczak/Navarre Performance Projects, is engaged in the dynamics of collaboration. Her practice includes listening for the unnoticed, the almost invisible and the very quiet.

We have worked together on two performance duets: *Control Signal*, which looks at pathways of electricity through our bodies, through our surroundings and through history, and *miles & miles*, a performance positioned at the edge of a landscape, with two people tied to opposite ends of a 100 metre rope.

Together, we have written this reflection on our making process that we liken to an ecosystem. We are suggesting that we are part of an ecosystem along with the elements of the place around us and the ideas we become aware of in it. We define the place around us as the world in which we imagine ourselves to be. It includes the very close and that which lies at an imagined distance as well as the reported realities we

---

1. www.goatislandperformance.org. Accessed 15 June 2021.

take on faith and the experience of life that we rely upon. We are not so much making work on the subject of ecology as we are activating an ecosystem through the way in which we go about working. Our method of working leaks its properties and makes itself felt in the body of the work composed.

Together, we are performing under the umbrella of Haranczak/Navarre Performance Projects.

For this essay, rather than blend our voices, we have each written complementary sections from our own points of view. These sections are preceded by our names as in a script for actors to speak.

Karen: We look for points of intersection

Haranczak/Navarre's work can be seen as research into collaborative experiences. With the meeting of more than one mind comes the possibility of surprise and misunderstanding – the resolution of which brings new clarity or opportunity for inspiration and unexpected solutions. Through collaboration, materials from separate minds with differing visions have to find a way to draw a connection between each other.

The content of each performance is determined through a process of discovery that allows the prevailing concerns and interests of the artists involved to be affected by the prevailing concerns and interests of the world around them. Historical, social, philosophical and cultural research and appropriation are considered alongside development of new text and movement.

We define performance theatre as a live event for the engagement of ideas, led by the bodily actions that we compose and perform. The audience are presented with a sequence of actions in order to follow a train of thought or succession of ideas. As distinct from more traditional theatre forms, which are often writer-led, performance theatre combines flexible forms of narrative with various forms of expression, through movement, sound, installation, materials and props.

Performers and audience together create a climate of attention that adjusts tempo and tunes thought processes on a communal level. Each individual audience member follows their own train of thought. The practice of paying attention for the duration of a performance deepens engagement with thinking processes, allowing time and space for the consideration of life through the themes of the performance. We are paying attention as a practice of social cooperation, a way of opening ourselves up to others, a practice of interdependence.

Karen: Collaboration, an ecology of mind

Collaboration invites the inclusion of multiple voices and exercises the ability to involve divergent viewpoints. I am using collaborative methods in support of practising restraint, tolerance and flexibility in responding to difference. In collaborative processes, we are listening for multiple answers to the questions we pose. We are not looking to find just the one answer that we hope fits all circumstances. Part of collaborating is allowing influences at play in the world around us to affect the direction of the work we make. We amble around for a while trying and testing where we are in relation to each other, our surroundings and our current interests as well as with the material that we bring to the moment. In performance, we find ourselves mostly occupied with preparing the ground for the purpose of optimal reception. We search for a context in which an idea can be heard – that is what we have to provide first for ourselves and then for the audience.

As a starting directive, we give ourselves the goal of listening to and sensing the environment in which we find ourselves. We are conscious that the conditions around us will feed into what the work becomes. The interaction between us creates a climate that will influence the work and its aesthetic. We are conscious that collaborative devising relies on a sensitivity to the ecology that we are part of as the work is being made – which is to say, to the totality or pattern of relations between the organisms involved and our environment. Some features of this support the work and some challenge it. Nevertheless, our ability to engage with these features is fundamental: they become the warp and the weft of what we are able to make. We begin with a kind of open intention, and we finish a work with fine tuning it to suit a set of specific intentions. In the vast middle area of the devising process, we are struggling to find the best way to interact with our immediate environment, and we are listening and observing what is possible within the parameters given. We have to find the balance between having an idea and uncovering what is there. We see ourselves as part of nature, as equal partners with the natural world we find ourselves surrounded by, even if that is a human-made construction. We might see ourselves as gardeners, but we also believe that the gardener is part of the garden.

The way of working is a steady movement forward and constant openness and attention to what is around us. When starting this process, we decided to allow ourselves to be contaminated by ideas and materials. We decided to not decide.

Throughout the process, we are collecting. It can be a thought, a piece of text, something that someone said or a recorded interaction between others. Why certain things are collected is hard to explain. It is as hard as trying to explain what happens in a chemical reaction. What is a 'gut feeling'? How do two people get excited about the same thing? What is collected is often something that is hard to understand. So we ask: How does that happen? Then, we each work to find our own way of answering it.

When these collections are put up against each other, they become combinations and patterns – a thread that sometimes stretches far and wide in order to catch itself at the other end. As Anne Boyman writes in the preface to *Earth Moves* by the architect Bernard Cache, it becomes 'a topography where a line is not what goes between two points, but a point is the intersection of many lines [...] it involves a flexible kind of continuity that is not totalized, finalized or closed'.[2]

It is like a wave: not one moment *nothing* and then the next *something*; it comes in a flux, a flow, an undertow. I am struggling to think about the slow build-up of material. The feeling of ideas not suddenly appearing from nowhere, from a void, but instead already being there from the beginning, latent and ready to disclose themselves. It is a slow layering of understanding and patient analysis of conversations and research.

We might perhaps imagine the process as something akin to the way that a wave leaves a tiny trace every time that it brushes onto the sand, until eventually a pattern is formed in the sand. Or the way, if you rub your fingertips against a wooden surface, slowly, over time, the skin will feel raw. Or, on staircases, where you see the indents caused by all the feet who stepped there before you, and you know they are only visible because it has happened so many times.

2. Anne Boyman, in preface to Bernard Cache (1995), *Earth Moves,
The Furnishing of Territories*, Boston, MA: MIT Press, p. xi.

Karen

Repetition creates a wear pattern, invisible as it manifests gradually, invisible to the insensible. The process is one of watching for wear patterns, of watching for the gradual, of waiting for the sense to sharpen. Materials have their own performance techniques and we tune in to them.

Sophie

The collected pieces of material, that before could seem blurry, suddenly stand out as something concrete as they start to connect with other pieces of material. The lines that connect the different ideas become visible. Now, we can start to pull them apart and to change their positions, looking for a better fit. We are alert to the unexpected – to what happens when a given piece of text is spoken in tandem with a series of movements. We note how the language of the movement merges with the language of the words and how the layer of understanding has now changed again.

Sophie: Structure, content, holes

We wrote down words on two large pieces of paper that illustrated, or articulated, what we were looking at in relation to the piece. They became a diagram describing our conversations. On one of the sheets of the paper, there were words associated with the structure of the piece; on the other, words associated with the content. At the point of writing the words, these two elements of the performance were distinctly separated.

It made me think about how an idea, even when it is tiny, fragile, almost non-existent, is still an idea, and how, if you keep looking, you will find something. Or that when something appears between us, we try to circle it from as many angles as possible, before we determine whether there is something we can or cannot use. The ecology of making is an unconscious process; we are not always aware of it; we let it happen to us.

Karen: A floor we might fall through

Our process for *Control Signal* was to pose a question and to follow the many answers provoked – to find a subject revealed in the material gathered. Working on the piece, we began with an interest in the interface of bodies and electricity, in the human desire to control our surroundings and in responding to the question 'what never stops?' The resulting work stands as a reflection on the cruelty brought down on disobedient subjects of capitalist mechanisms (Topsy the elephant, electrocuted by Thomas Edison), on hysterical authoritarian states (Ethel Rosenberg, executed by a 1950s' American state made hysterical by McCarthy era anti-communism) and on a series of vibrations and reverberations of past events that never quite go away but ricochet through time and our bodies for as long as we carry on. We conceive of these resonances as avenues of electricity both inside and outside the body, laying paths and leaving residues.

Following a successful run of *Control Signal*, Sophie and I began work on a new duet, *miles & miles*, where we pared back our approach by starting with purely formal concerns: a system of containment interrupted by periods of its inverse or opposite. It – the system – might be thought of as a set of containers for alternating states of control and chaos. It might be considered as a holding vessel for something like water that, without a container, has no shape of its own and disappears through whatever avenues allow it to follow gravity to the lowest place. Or, perhaps, a floor that holds us up but which has places we fall through, and this instability contributes to the content carried by the form. We started with form in order to cast about searching for a content uniquely suited.

Material is required to activate the form, and in devising sessions, we provoked material in the service of this form. We spent weeks alone together, just the two of us, bashing through techniques for generating material, making performance directives, researching ideas involving loops and fugues and mystifying mathematical propositions. We came across the statement 'this statement is unprovable', and this tickled our brains and made us feel we were getting somewhere. But how do you know you are getting somewhere when the way has not been signposted and there isn't a road map for where you are going? When control is relinquished, outcomes are untestable.

In the absence of giving up, eventually some figures start to emerge through the mist. Sometimes, this means we recognized a destination as we arrived, and at other times, it means we did not know where we had ended up. With diligence something eventually emerges, and then, the question to ask becomes: 'Regardless of what expectations might have been, do we like where we have ended up?'

What happens in the studio in a devising process can feel like a mystery. But the process has definable and readable boundaries or guidelines if you make them. Defining our methods as a conscious act of conversation is a very important part of the way we work together. We try to assume as little as possible and to pose as many questions as we can, especially around points of disagreement. Questions slow things down and answers help keep the misery of miscommunication at a minimum.

You make a seal with an individual or a series of individuals, and this seal creates a spontaneous contract that writes itself according to the chemistry between you. As you work together in a studio, you sense and test what the rules of this contract are. You discover what is possible.

As I have been working with a small number of different people on duets in recent years, I have learnt that working dynamics vary considerably with each partner. I find that I am a different creature with different people; my palate of responses calibrated to what I perceive in the gap between us.

Karen: Why we do work-in-progress performances

The work needs access to the public, to be contaminated by opinion and the unfamiliar. The magic here is that people do not have to say anything in order for us to get a sense of what is happening in the work. In this invisible and affective process of feedback, the piece is now clearer and more legible than it was previously.

However, when the audience do speak in post-show discussions or otherwise, and regardless of the sense their comments make, it always makes us think. But here we have to be careful. We have to continue to listen to our own convictions even as we happily take on board what our responders have to tell us. We have to remember that we are more intimate with the piece than they are and that what they are telling us is that we have to bridge a gap, to get closer to them. There is intimacy we still have to bring. There are many different ways to approach this task, and only some of them break our hearts. We move towards the ones that do not.

Karen: Post-show discussions that draw out articulations
we did not know we had

Tom, a third-year student at the University of Falmouth, was writing his dissertation around the idea of the compositional ordering of a performance piece and was very interested in the way that we chose to order and compose the various 'micro-elements' within *Control Signal*. In an email, he wrote,

> At the beginning of the piece the different elements seemed quite clearly defined around the edges and did not appear to relate to each other in any obvious way. However as the performance went on they slowly began to spill over into each other. I particularly remember the first moment that 'Ethel Rosenberg' was mentioned and the way that that sort of seeped/trickled/conducted into the other elements of the piece, almost like electricity, making connections in my brain which began to join all of these individual elements together. Fantastic!

His question was,

> How much 'control' did you exercise over this spilling over? Was the order meticulously planned for these spillages to happen at certain times? Or do you feel that this was more something that was out of your 'control'?

I responded that it was, as he put it, 'meticulously planned', but it was also intuitively felt and, at the same time, out of our control. The style in which we worked on the performance meant that there was a lot of trial and error. We had to find out how to place little, time-released capsules here and there, at the beginning and through the middle of the performance. So that when the 'big ideas' are introduced, it feels like there is already a history for them to rest on or to activate. It causes the piece to assemble inside the heads of the audience. I think of it as little bits of dried moss that spring to life when watered.

Another student asked a related question during the post-show discussion. He asked about how the idea of translating internal thoughts into performance material related to the apparently fragmentary nature of the show. Sequencing the material is the most important thing we do. And this is specifically related to how we convey thoughts from the tumult of information in our heads into aesthetic facts. Translating thought into material that can be shared with other people, even people we have never met, is a tricky business. It is easy if the thoughts can be generalized and concretized, but if we want them to be re-assembled inside the heads of each audience member according to their own inclinations, then it is a delicate balance. Maybe it is like putting model ships inside bottles. It should not be possible, but it is. It is a way of making the reading of the show belong to the audience, because they participate in the assembling of the set of ideas that the performance has evoked.

Beginning to make our new piece, *miles & miles*, we decided to start with an idea for a structure, a structure of falling in and out of the performance, of having two states alternating – one contained and 'known' and the other un-contained and 'unknown'. We decided that these un-contained moments could be seen as 'holes', something you fall into, and a place where anything could happen. We determined that those moments should be improvized, coming as a surprise to both of us, requiring us to negotiate in the moment.

We thought about the fragility of the performance moment – of two people finding out as they go along. I asked, 'how do two performers keep surprising each other, hold the line taut and then accept holes in the line? In what ways can people challenge the point where the edge does not exist?'

At this point, these descriptions were merely conceptual thoughts; they described the sensation of the performance, of the piece. For a long time, we were frustrated. Too much talking; not enough making.

We made performance directives for each other – written tasks to generate material. The tasks were specific or open-ended, and after a short amount of time to prepare something, we showed them to each other. Here is one example of a directive leading to the creation of a performative fragment: What is the relationship between inner and outer landscapes? Make a restriction for yourself by creating an edge.

In the material created as a response to this directive, Karen spoke of an element from the Alfred Hitchcock movie *Spellbound* (1945) – a film where a man falls into fugue states of amnesia. She suggested that we watch it, and afterwards, we started to think about loops, amnesia, vertigo, cliffs, fragility, future, past, Ingrid Bergman and Alfred Hitchcock, being stuck, competition, climbing, being saved and wanting to save. The movie had become a springboard, something that other things could leap from and coalesce around. The film became central to composing our material, but we could just as well have started somewhere else completely different. It is not always the intentionally sought after material that ends up in the piece; sometimes, something appears out of the blue.

Sophie: A layer

Once you have spoken about an idea, what happens then? What image do you choose as a vehicle to carry thought? Where does the next layer come in? What is a layer? We start to find examples. We start to find carriers of information, subjects of stories. And if these stories come from people who live or have lived in the real world, their stories already hold a layer or background that we do not fabricate.

That story holds a background, an upbringing, a culture, a way of speaking, a way of looking at the world. When we use someone's experience, it becomes a layer, stretching itself out beyond the rehearsal room. Like an ecology, it is bigger than us. Let us pretend that the story is a crop, a plant. You have the stem, and then, you start to separate the wheat from the chaff. This leaves you with a pile of the grains that you have picked. You can start to use the grains for something, but whatever it ends up being, it still holds within it the memory of being a plant, of having been harvested, of having been in contact with you.

Karen: In the room of the devising process

What is it to spend time in a room with someone with only the rules that we make up together? Each time is native to those two. You have to step into that hazard zone to discover the result. We find it important to work by working rather than working by talking about working. Ideas should come in as performative fragments and be shown rather than described. In this way, the work is drawn into the room, realized in time and place. Once it is brought into the space, the material might be different from what it was as it rested inside one of our heads. Its activation in time and space allows us both to respond to the same material. In this way, our differing viewpoints do not get in the way as long as we agree on the material itself.

In the course of the devising process, we have to be clear about heading somewhere without really knowing or narrowing down where that is until the work shows us – the work is a living organism. We also have to renounce clinging to preconceived notions. And when the end of the work comes, we have to find a way of loving it, even if it is not what we had expected or hoped for.

I am effectively talking about letting the performance be what it is, even if it means we cannot take all of the credit for it ourselves. The work comes as a surprise, something we found rather than something we made. It is about an ecological way of living and making – it is about relinquishing control and opening yourself up to the environment, to something that is not you – a kind of non-human at the very heart of the human.

Sophie: The moment something is performed and lost

At the end of *miles & miles*, Karen performs a text in which she asks whether what we are doing in that moment is a performance or the record of the performance.

It can sometimes feel like that, in the moment, when you are performing, perhaps even more so when it is a work-in-progress. As the material is so raw and fragile, you are constantly looking for the words and movements. You know it, but you also do not know it, so you have to be able to look for it while performing it. You lose control. You are aware that your movements and words are now with them, the audience. They, the words, are lingering in the space, out of your possession – and are now residing in the 'ear-brains' of the audience. You move on, thinking about the next moment, but cannot quite grasp it, and so you think back to the last moment, and you cannot quite grasp that either. But you are there, and what happens is what you do. Always, what you do. And you, in this case, is plural, multiple.

Sophie: A negotiation

Everything is allowed only in so far as it has been negotiated in and through our whole collaboration. This is the negotiation that has taken place in each and every rehearsal, in each conversation. Although we cannot lean back into our material, because we do not know it that well yet, we can always lean back into each other. And the action of leaning into each other might well be where the whole thing comes to life. It is the immediate dynamic between the two performers, something that will develop with time, with patience and with the work that is put into it.

We say that the ecosystem of the studio in which we work influences the outcome of the performance directives we compose as much as the responses of audiences and other outside eyes do and our own aesthetic sense of what we intend does. Karen says none of it happens without the fermentation our ideas undergo as a result of exposure to what is in the air around us. The climate of attention we need for the composition of our work comes from finding a context in which our ideas can be heard. *We are finding this context by making it.*[3]

3. This references a motto which previously appeared on Goat Island's website: 'We found a performance by making it'.

When we began working together, Karen said to me that the ideas created while working with someone do not belong solely to either person. They arise because of the very cosmos that we have built through our process. In order for the day to continue, for the collaboration to flow, we create space for one another to be.

There is a struggle here between independence and interdependence. The need to have someone else with you, if you are to go on. Collaboration becomes a way of thinking – a practice. And I can feel how this approach to another person extends into my other relationships, becoming an ecology, a process of relating, a mode of being and becoming.

It is like those moments when you can see that someone wants to say something, but they do not know how to articulate it. And they stop themselves, perhaps. And they say, 'oh, maybe it does not matter'. And then you say, 'no, it does matter'.

It always matters because that next sentence might be an important one. Without the other, thoughts are diminished, half of what they could be. With the other, thoughts and ideas travel to places where you could not go alone.

This is an edited version of an essay of the same name, originally published in 'Performance and Ecology: What Can Theatre Do?' a special issue of the journal *Green Letters: Studies in Ecocriticism*, 2016, 20:3, 10.1080/14688417.2016.1191996. Accessed 24 December 2020.

Not so much balanced as balancing (miles & miles)

MARY PATERSON

Before it starts, the woman next to me asks, in a tense whisper, *Is it real?* Our elbows are touching, our eyes are looking forwards and our concentration is on the two women standing on a piece of wood that is balanced on a brick at the front of the stage.

Is it real?

Here we are, elbows touching, eyes forward. There they are, elbows touching, eyes forward.

Dark hair, dark clothes, sensible shoes. Bodies touching, gently, as if for reassurance or as if jostling for space. Not so much balanced, actually, as balancing. Legs shaking. Skin touching, as if jostling for space is the closest thing to reassurance, as if proximity is a kind of safeguard.

There they are. Each of them tied to one end of a coil of rope: one at the waist, one at the ankle. Each tied to the other as if they are ready to –

What's the word for it? That feeling – when your feet shuffle closer to the edge and your eyes look down and you think you might – ?

Here we are. There they are. Each of them tied to one end of a rope that is suspended from a metal hook hanging from the ceiling. *Is it real?* Thick rope. Old rope. The kind of thick, old rope that will burn your skin right off as it slips through your fingers. Elbows touching, eyes forward, holding onto something that is going to hurt.

In unison, they step off the piece of wood that is balancing on a brick; eyes forward, as if they are not dependent on one another for the act of unbalancing, as if they are not tethered to one another while time trails messily behind them. Separately, they wander round the room; eyes forward, as if they are individuals, as if being an individual is a possibility, as if being alone is a material reality, like a belt or a film or the edge of the world. The rope ravels after them like a memory.

Is it real?

Here we are. Unbalanced. Tied in knots. What's the word? When your feet edge closer and you can't tell the difference between a gesture of companionship and a competition of proximity and the prelude to a push and – ?

Eyes forward, elbows touching. There she is. Speaking into a microphone, speaking in the voice of a half forgotten movie star and a scientist and a story you heard on the radio while you were eating your breakfast, lifting the spoon to your mouth with a silent rhythm as if you can stall for time before the day starts to ask its normal questions. There they are, speaking in casual voices to each other; eyes forward, as if this is not a matter of life and death,

as if their ankles, their waists and their elbows are not within touching distance, as if this whole matter of beginnings and endings and being entangled is not a landscape of invisible precipices but something man-made like a stage. Is it real? One of them says, 'nice navigation', and the other one nods, as if the route she has taken all round the edges of the room was the answer to a question that hasn't yet been –

Are you the kind of person who will find yourself walking up the tallest thing you can see? (The steps, the cliff, the soft, purple hill of your memories.) And when you get there, are you the kind of person who will feel your toes slide right to the edge? And then, are you the kind of person who will shut your eyes into the fresh breeze beckoning you from below? To breathe it in – this cool, clean, unusual air? And then, are you the kind of person who will reach out for something to hold onto?

Is it real?

They tug the past behind them as they turn. It whips elegant shapes into the air and collapses in knots. They rush to the front of the stage and dance. Two women, eyes forward, hands shaking (sometimes), bodies moving (quickly), as if they are being moved by something like a memory. They separate. One person rocks backwards

and forwards on a squeak in a floorboard. One person speaks the words of a man in the flat planes of a white stretch at the edge of the world. One person reads out plans for beginnings and endings and middles, as if this is not an event but a never-ending rehearsal, as if she is not on a flat, wide, man-made stage but inside a vast, white waiting room perched on a cliff at the edge of –

And when you reach out, will you reach out instinctively or will you curl your tongue round some words, to ask for something? And will you use your own voice or borrow someone else's?

Is it real?

Here we are.

Wandering across the clifftops of a wide, flat waiting room that no one else can see. Here we are, rocking backwards and forwards on a floorboard that groans under the pressure; here we are, arranging our limbs in the shape of a person

falling, a person suspended in the act of descent, a person training for the unknown, a person who knows that when it happens, all the preparation with the rope and the skin and the balancing and the words will be a kind of –

Here we are.

One of us concentrates her eyes and her finger tips on the effort not to –

Eyes forward. Remaining, remaining, remaining, remaining –

And when you reach out, what will you find to hold onto? (A memory, a burden, a razor-sharp ledge.) And will you grip it so tightly that you hear it rip? (Your balance, your memory, your fingertips.) And will it rip until the tough brown hide of a rope or an arm caught in the flat dawn sun is waving against a powder blue sky or a burnt yellow rock or a bottomless pit, depending on your view? And are you the kind of person who likes to plan how this is going?

Here we are. Tied in knots,

the past whipping itself into shapes that other people can see. The past curling itself into messy knots, and there's nothing we're going to do about it but choose whether to secure our memories to our bellies or our feet. Eyes forward, gazing at the horizon, real, imagined or as seen on TV, as if our minds are not a vast white expanse but a landscape of cliff tops, edges and long, dark, bottomless –

Is it real?

Here we are. Holding on. Waiting, waiting, waiting, waiting for the horizon to come close enough to touch it with our fingertips, tie it round our waists and trail it behind us like a good story. Is it real? Here we are, bowing our heads and lifting our feet, unravelling, heels pushing into groaning wood, toes falling into –

Here we are.

Balancing, balancing, balancing –

Mary Paterson saw *miles & miles* on 7 July 2016,
at Chisenhale Dance Space, London.

The Collaborative Artistic Working Process of Control Signal: A Drama-Linguistic Exploration of the Shifting of Roles

ANDREA MILDE

1. Introduction

Figure 1: Karen and Sophie are jointly developing the script for *Control Signal*.
Karen's studio, Hackney Wick, East London (08/2013) (Image: AM).

What is going on when two performance artists jointly create a performance
piece from scratch? What are the features of their collaborative performance-
making process? How do the two performers communicate their ideas, thoughts
and comments, and how do they make decisions? In this chapter, I will explore
from a discursive perspective, supported by video-ethnography, what is going on
during the studio working process when the two performers, Karen Christopher
(K), founder of Haranczak/Navarre Performance Projects, and Sophie Grodin (S),
collaboratively create *Control Signal*. Their working process is embedded in the context
of a series of duets that were part of a multi-year project by the company Haranczak/
Navarre Performance Projects. I have observed that in their studio time – a face-
to-face artistic working process during which work is devised – working means
communicating, and much of this is spoken. In the studio, K and S use movement,
dance, gestures, props, sound, rhythm, writing, drawing, translating and elements of
language learning in their collaborative devising process, and all these activities are
intertwined with spoken communication.

The way I carry out my ethnographic fieldwork, investigation, and how I present my findings on their authentic spoken communication is based on the *linguistics in drama* approach that I have developed for investigating communication in collaborative artistic and creative working processes, in particular for theatre, drama and performance arts contexts (Milde 2019, 2012, 2007a, b, c).

In this chapter, I demonstrate the process of the *shifting of roles* as a key feature of the joint devising process, based on empirical examples, and will show how this becomes apparent by investigating K's and S's conversations as part of their working process and by analyzing transcribed extracts of their conversations. The examples are taken from the ethnographic fieldwork that I carried out during the performance-making process of *Control Signal* in 2013.

The basis of my *linguistics in drama* approach is that reformulation, along with turn-taking, is one of the key organizing structures in the collaborative spoken text-production process. Reformulation, by which I mean formulating a piece of spoken text again by altering the previous text version, occurs in different ways depending on each group's or individual's practice, availability, experience, time, budget constraints and so on. My method for investigating and analyzing talk in drama processes draws on the research areas of spoken discourse analysis, text-production and *critique génétique* (French manuscript research, cf. Grésillon 1999) and in turn contributes to these areas as well as to drama practice research and creativity research. The communication in studio and rehearsal processes is observable, but until recently, these processes have been a sort of a black box (Milde 2019, 2012, 2007a, b, c). During K's and S's studio working process, an interactive situation, both reformulation and turn-taking as organizing structures, can be observed while the two collaborators reveal activities such as giving feedback, reading out loud something written that might become part of the script and sharing ideas.

In this chapter,[1] I demonstrate how the different elements the two collaborators integrate into their performance-making process and the way they communicate about it provide insight into this duet's performance-making practice and probably (this would need further investigation) into the artistic practice of Haranczak/Navarre Performance Projects.

---

1. I am drawing on the presentation and panel discussion Karen, Sophie and I had during the keynote discussion at the performance symposium *Of Two Minds* (2014), University of Roehampton, in partnership with Sadler's Wells, when our discussion focused around the selected three features of reformulation, shift of roles and orientation points.

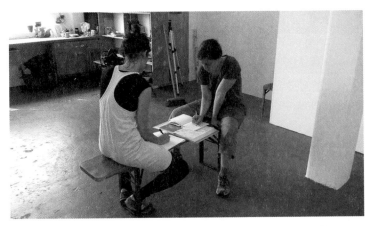

Figure 2: The two collaborators writing down their ideas. Karen's studio, Hackney Wick (08/2013) (Image: AM).

Figure 3: The two collaborators working on their movements. Karen's studio, Hackney Wick (08/2013) (Image: AM).

In the process of devising *Control Signal*, there are parts of the studio working process that – at first sight – contain no spoken language. For instance, when both collaborators work on writing down their ideas (Figure 2) or when working on movements (Figure 3). These parts are part of the overall working process, which involves a lot of talk, either before the collaborators start writing things down or interspersed with it (i.e. they discuss, write, discuss and write again). If we want to understand as fully as possible what is going on in any part of the production of *Control Signal*, we need to be able to see it in the context of the overall working process (cf. Grésillon 1999), and if conversations between the collaborators are an essential element of this process, then we need to be able to investigate their spoken communication.

Data

The data used in this chapter come from one data set, based on the performance-making process that took place in Karen's former studio in East London (Figures 1–3) in early August 2013. The first example comes from the first day of my fieldwork, and the second example comes from the second day of my fieldwork. The performance-making process during that time involved the two collaborators. On the second day, they had someone come in to view an extract of their working process and give some feedback. I was in the space with the collaborators for the entire time of the recording.

When I started investigating selected sequences of my recordings of Karen's and Sophie's communication during their studio work, an important step was to transcribe their conversations, which is a common practice in disciplines that study spoken language such as Spoken Discourse Analysis (e.g. Cameron 2001) and Conversational Analysis (Schegloff et al. 1977). There are different transcription models for producing transcriptions, and some disciplines are more open-minded about different transcription models than others. The transcription system I draw on for transcribing sequences of the communication during a collaborative text-production process in the performance arts, or an artistic working process, is based on the musical notation system (*Partiturschreibweise*) that Konrad Ehlich and Jochen Rehbein first introduced in the German-speaking Spoken Discourse Analysis world in the 1970s (Ehlich and Rehbein 1976).

I find this transcription model particularly useful for creative and artistic settings as it allows the reader to get an easily readable overview of simultaneous communication between multiple participants in a space and accommodates transcription of longer sequences. One may have the most useful fieldnotes, sufficient ethnographic material, to make sense of the situation in which the language was used (here, for performance-making) and have viewed or listened to the selected sequences many times, but in my experience, when transcribing the sequences, new aspects of the communication become audible or visible. It is my aim in this chapter to produce transcriptions that are easy to read. I have observed many themes, such as 'orientation points', 'looking at the drawing' and 'collaborative script writing', during the production process of *Control Signal*. In this chapter, I focus on the feature of 'shift of roles'.

Figure 4: Hackney Wick; location of Karen's studio (08/2013) (Image: AM).

Figure 5: Building in which Karen's studio is located, Hackney Wick (08/2013) (Image: AM).

Figure 6: The two collaborators in Karen's studio, Hackney Wick (08/2013) (Image: AM).

Method

How does one investigate the face-to-face working process of performance artists? There are different ways of doing this, depending on the particular aim of the investigation. The focus of my approach (*linguistics in drama*) is on the face-to-face text-development process, and, as mentioned above, this can be influenced by other factors (such as availability of participants or space). Drama and other performance arts processes such as rehearsals and studio work are complex and can appear messy. For example, collaborators working on a new idea in the studio can appear chaotic, but there is usually an underlying structure and purpose.

For many years, people in the world of drama, theatre, performance and arts have been asking me about what to look for when investigating drama working processes. In response to this, I developed the ten categories[2] (Figure 7) as a way into approaching rehearsals and studio working processes. My fieldwork on *Control Signal* confirmed that these communicative sub-activities are also useful in collaborative studio working processes. As drama and other performance arts processes are closely intertwined with spoken communication, it is essential to take specific communicative activities into account (for activity types and language, see Levinson 1992).

These categories are not meant to be used in a prescriptive way, and I do not think that artists need to worry about the communicative sub-activities when creating work. The ten categories might be useful though for purposes such as critical reflection of one's own artistic practice, analyzing someone else's artistic practice, teaching in educational institutions or consulting. This list is not exhaustive but represents the main groups of sub-activities that I have identified as relevant in the artistic text-development processes that I investigated and have personally come across during working processes. As mentioned before, my research is empirically based, and my findings and examples are based on observation, not on theoretical construction.

2. Professor Ben Rampton at King's College London was the first person (during my time as Visiting Scholar at the Centre for Language, Discourse & Communication, KCL in 2011) to encourage me to write these categories down. I would like to thank Karen Christopher and also Kristine Landon-Smith and Tamasha Theatre for their long-term interest and openness towards my research, which helped me to develop the ten categories, among other things.

Category	Sub-activities	Essential Questions	Examples
1	Using a script	In what way is a script being used? Is it ready-made or is it being developed?	A Shakespeare text is used for an exercise. An improvisation is used to create the script for a scene.
	Scripting text	In what way is text scripted within the process? Is a scripted text provided during the working process (that wasn't provided beforehand)?	Performers write down the details of a dialogue after having developed it from scratch.
2	Providing feedback	In what way is feedback provided? What sort of feedback? By whom? For whom? Does it include a suggestion (see category 10)?	'ok . right . great . that is (?) really .. it's very excellent' 'if you let the text guide you instead of you controlling the text you're slightly closed'
3	Providing explanations	In what way are explanations provided?	'the reason why I want the language people .. largely . to do it . is because I .. ultimately we are saying you're coming from foreign lands to London'
	Providing (background) information	In what way is information provided?	'you've been on this ship you've got off'
4	Using improvisations	In what way are improvisations being used? Are there instructions for them (see category 5)? Are the improvisations keyed or totally open?	'we're going to do tiny little improvisation and move into it'

Figure 7: Ten communicative sub-activities within devising- or directing-conversations in drama/ performance arts processes (Milde 2012, 2019; Milde et al. 2014).

Category	Sub-activities	Essential Questions	Examples
5	Providing instructions and using keys as a way of providing instructions	In what way are instructions being used? In what way are keys being used? Are the keys for how to do something, or for what to do? Is a sub-text provided? Has a suggestion been made through a kind of description (e.g. through a scenario or a kind of demonstration)? Are cues being given? Are text parts being conducted (as a kind of 'live instructing')?	'you're just going to be that guy doing a bit of your beat box thing' 'you think it's great'
6	Framing one's own activity	In what way do drama practitioners (e.g. directors) frame their directing-activities? What does it indicate?	'what you're going to do' 'what I want you to do'
7	Sharing ideas, thoughts, stories, anecdotes, etc.	In what way is the sharing of ideas, thoughts, stories, etc. being used? Is the sharing of ideas etc. aimed at providing feedback (see category 2), information (see category 3), or suggestions (see category 10)?	'My sister used to do this too'
8	Acting out/ performing a version	In what way is the acting out/the performing of a text version being used? By whom? For whom?	((Shakespeare text)) *it is the cause! . it is the cause my soul*
9	Providing/ asking questions	In what way are questions being used? Are they rhetorical questions? Are they aimed at giving feedback (see category 2) or suggestions (see category 10)?	'am I doing it from here?'
10	Providing/ making suggestions	In what way are suggestions being used? Are they aimed at providing feedback (see category 2) or sharing an idea (see category 7)?	'I could do it more quickly'

How to use the table with the ten categories

During the *Control Signal* working process, there were times when Karen and Sophie were sitting down and writing (Figures 1 and 2). To investigate one of Karen's and Sophie's writing activities, you could do the following:

- In the sub-activities column in the table, look for the activities that involve writing and working on scripts (within the studio work process). That would be category 1.

- Now choose the most relevant activity within this sub-activity, if there is more than one. You might decide on the activity of *scripting text.* In the middle column of Essential Questions, you will find questions that will give you some ideas about what to look out for and help you to start off your investigation. Also, check if the activity in the example seems similar to the activities you are dealing with.

- You can also use the table from the right to the left. For instance, if you are unsure whether you are dealing with a particular communicative activity (e.g. Karen was performing/reading a sequence of the script she had produced), have a look at several examples on the right side and see if any other examples are similar to what you are dealing with.

- If you found an example that seems to demonstrate a similar activity to what you are dealing with (you might find that the example of category 8 seems to be similar), you will then find relevant questions in the middle column and can then look up on the left what the overall communicative activity is (*acting out/ performing a version*).

This will hopefully have given some orientation to anyone who would like to use the table of ten communicative sub-activities for understanding or investigating performance arts production processes.

While carrying out fieldwork during the performance-making process of *Control Signal* in 2013, one of my most memorable observations was how often there were moments of surprising, unpredictable change that were somehow closely intertwined with the collaboration process (and not a random solo activity). I noticed that this was somehow initiated by Karen, but in a way that seemed to challenge herself at least as much as Sophie. It looked to me as though it was aimed at ensuring that both collaborators remained equally involved and responsible within the working process. When I took a closer look at some of my data a few months later, I realized that the shifting of the performers' roles played an important part in these surprise moments, which I wanted to investigate more closely at some point.

I noticed how in these surprise moments Karen seemed to shake things up in order to keep the collaboration in a flow and in balance.

In the following section, I will present two examples of the various ways that roles are swapped and changed during Karen's and Sophie's performance-making process. I will explore this by looking at two extracts from two conversations that took place between the two collaborators in Karen's studio.

I will demonstrate how the shifting of roles appears to be an important feature in the collaborators' swapping of roles while creating the performance piece *Control Signal*. For the performers, creating a performance piece involves communicating their ideas to each other and giving each other feedback. I will discuss the feature of the shifting of roles by looking at the face-to-face conversation of the two collaborators, exploring how both Karen and Sophie suggest things to each other, how they respond and how they explain what they are doing.

Example 1: Shifting roles: practising Danish

The following example shows an extract from the face-to-face working practice of two performers who bring very different experiences, ideas, knowledge and skills into this working process. The performers had worked on an earlier version of this piece about a year previously, when they also performed it. They are in Karen's studio and gather what they can remember from a year ago, decide on what they want to keep and develop new ideas and material for *Control Signal*. It is the first day of their studio work of this particular working phase. It is 5 August 2013,

Figure 8: Karen repeats Danish words after Sophie, while also trying to remember them from a year ago. Karen's studio, Hackney Wick (08/2013) (Image: AM).

about 11.20 a.m.; it is already fairly hot outside and inside of the studio and the performers are about one hour and fourteen minutes into their working process. The extract shown below lasts almost three minutes.

This extract from a longer conversation demonstrates how Karen brings about a shift of their roles within the performance-making process and the performance, and why.

Participants are (in alphabetical order) as follows. K = Karen. S = Sophie. T stands for translation[3] from Danish into English. For transcription conventions, see the Appendix.

3. I would like to thank my colleague Randi Benedikte Brodersen, University of Bergen, Norway, for transcribing the Danish elements and translating it into English for me. I am solely responsible for the transcription and its organization.

01 K: *. ham*   *. eller hende selv*   *. til*
02 S: [...] *ham*   *. eller hende selv*   *. til at.*
03 T: him   or herself   to

04 K: ((is getting a bit stuck)) *. at få . at få vasket si . ine hænder+* I know I almost
05 S: *at få vasket sine hænder*
06 T: to have one's hands washed

07 K: ((laughing)) got it+   *til at få*   *vasket*   *sine*
08 S: *til at få*   *. vasket*   *. sine*   *.*
09 T: to have   washed   his/her

10 K: *hænder*   ((laughing)) except there was one word at a time+
11 S: *hænder*   *.. ja*   *er der en*   *er der en*
12 T: hands   yes   is there someone

13 K: *er der en*   *. der vil vælge*   *. ham*   *.*
14 S: *. der vil vælge*   *. ham*   *. eller hende selv . til*
15 T: who will choose   him   or herself   to

16 K: *til*   *. at få vasket*   *. sine hænder*
17 S: *. at få vasket*   *. sine hænder*
18 T: have one's hands washed   her/his hands

19 K: *.*   we better write that down
20 S: I thought (?) and then we like   (??) yeah   and then we're like

21 K: and then yeah I said *.*
22 S: *.. det skal være nu* ((and laughs)) *hehe+*
23 T: that must be now

24 K: *det skal være nu .* ((laughing)) and your friends all laughed .. everyone else
25 S: X((Sophie hides head on table top and laughs quietly)) 'he

26 K: was bemused 'hehe'+   alright . so   of course
27 S: he'+   hopefully ..   (do?) I write it? . no? .

28 K: yeah .   but we don't need (the truth is?) we don't need to write it down
29 S: ok .   but you write it . you (want?) to write it

30 K: again . because the fact is that I do have it . and the thing is . for me . if I
31 S: ok (??)   ok

32 K: just can go back to that same .. if it's slightly different . it's going . to really
33 S: yeah   and then look at it   yeah

34 K: throw me   ..   so it's better if I . go back to the memorized (?) the same one
35 S: yeah

36 K: I did   you know and that was like . a year ago .   I haven't done
37 S: ((yawning)) yeah+ .   ((smiles)) hm+

38 K: it in more than a year
39 S: . but that's why I'm saying you're so good . because

40 K: yeah . I'm not that good . but let's
41 S: it actually you . you almost had it without   ((disagreeing)) NO . but

42 K: ((in disbelief)) yeah yeah yeah+ . but let's hope I'll get . a little bit better yeah
43 S: it's a year ago+.

44 K: because .   I kept looking at my . my 'ch' . then .. but uhm
45 S: you will be   but you will

46 S: just have to practise . and we will just practise e-ver-y day. but it's also fun

47 K: no no no I will I will probably never be that good .
48 S: when you're not so good .   but

49 K: but I think I at least need to know it . it'll be the pronunciation that's a little off

50 K: . but it'll also be . I think for me the important thing is .. u:h that in some
51 S: yeah

52 K: way I'm a little bit . effaced . by it
53 S: what is effaced? (??like) mean uh . in the

54 K: in the performance   so that . like
55 S: performance or just now?   yeah

56 K: self-effacement is . is is kind of you know uh ((makes a clicking sound with

57 K: tongue)) 't'+ . taking off your protection you know   you're becoming quite
58 S: yeah   yeah

59 K: vulnerable   . uhm . or even you you're sort of downgrading . yourself
60 S: exactly   yeah

61 K: a little bit . so .. for me . that's the important . part of me saying it . so I don't
62 S: yeah

63 K: want to be completely confident   but I DO want to be able to actually say it
64 S: no

65 K: . uhm . but I think just the fact that I don't know any other Danish.
66 S: yeah

67 K: ((laughing)) and that I have to remember it exactly+ . that's gonna do that
68 S: ((laughing)) hm+

69 K: uhm . cause it's quite a strange thing to speak . words that . you've only
70 S: yeah

71 K: been taught   mean something   but you haven't actually tested them
72 S: yes   yeah   ((humorously)) I could

73 K: I know
74 S: have said a:nything+

The part of their conversation that takes place immediately before this extract shows that they are both jointly trying to remember the exact Danish wording from the script they had used in their performance a year before. In the extract, they continue working on the Danish phrases, as we can see from line 01 to line 16 (the starting point here would be category 1 if one wanted to use the ten categories). In the extract above, we can see that S teaches K some Danish words and phrases. When the phrase is rather long and K is struggling a bit to repeat it in one go without hesitation (in line 04: . *at få . at få vasket si . ine hænder*), S breaks up the same phrase into smaller units for K (in line 08: *til at få*) and they continue. K reflects in a humorous and relaxed way on how she is getting on with the Danish so far (in lines 04 and 07: *I know I almost ((laughing)) got it+*, and in line 10: *((laughing)) except there was one word at a time+*). Once they have practised this section of Danish, S talks about which Danish phrase is coming next (in lines 20 and 22) and K talks about wanting to write down the phrases they just practised (line 19), before realizing that she has already written it down (in lines 28 and 30). K then mentions (in lines 32, 34 and 36: *if it's slightly different . it's going . to really throw me .. so it's better if I . go back to the memorized (?) the same one I did*) that in order to make the Danish language sequence work for her in the performance, she wants to use the script they had already developed and used a year ago. S (in lines 45 and 46: *but you will just have to practise . and we will just practise e-ver-y day*) responds to K by suggesting that they will just have to practise the Danish language sequence every day now. K points out (in line 50: *I think for me the important thing is .. uuh that in some way I'm a little bit . effaced . by it*, and in lines 57 and 59: *you're becoming quite vulnerable*) that the main reason for using the Danish language sequence is to become vulnerable in the performance (in lines 54 and 55). K also adds that she does not want to be completely confident with it (in lines 61 and 63).

In the example above, different types of voices become apparent, and I will just mention three of them. In the transcription, we can see the collaborators' voices that become visible when they are developing and discussing their work (e.g. in lines 41 and 43: *but it's a year ago*). There are the performers' voices when the collaborators enact a piece of text from their script or while developing their script (e.g. in line 1: *eller hende selv*). Towards the end of the transcribed extract above, another voice becomes apparent. It is the voice of the artist or the practitioner who reveals an approach, a practice or a certain way of doing things (e.g. in lines 50 and 52: *I think for me the important thing is .. u:h that in some way I'm a little bit . effaced . by it*). Voice is used here in the Bakhtinian sense (Bakhtin 1984) and means perspective, which, in this context, is the perspective of the artistic practitioner. It shows us K's practice to impose a challenge on herself with something she (K) is not experienced with while S, her collaborator, can get on with something she (S) is very experienced and confident in.

This example demonstrates two different ways that *a shift of roles* can be integrated in the collaborators' working process. The first way that a role swap occurs during this extract has an impact on the studio working process. The role swap that takes place through the use of Danish creates more of a balance of power between the two and has the effect that S, the less experienced performer, has the role of the confident and experienced one, whereas K, the more experienced performer, does not know any Danish, needs to find a way of delivering it and is completely reliant on S's knowledge and support. S acknowledges her power when saying that she could have passed anything off as Danish to Karen (in lines 72 and 74: *I could have said a:nything*).

The other type of shift of roles has an impact on their work during the performance, which K talks about in lines 50 to 63. This role swap uses Danish language as a self-imposed vulnerability with the aim of not being 'completely confident' in the performance.

Here is another example of how a shift of roles occurs in the studio working process.

Example 2: Shifting roles: do you want to *try* it?

The following example shows an extract from the face-to-face of K's and S's working process in Karen's studio. They are trying out ideas and sections of the script for *Control Signal*, which they have worked on earlier. It is the second day of their studio work of this particular working phase. It is 6 August 2013; it is already fairly hot outside and inside of the studio and the performers are several hours into their working process as it is afternoon. The following extract lasts about 31 seconds.

This extract is taken from a longer conversation and demonstrates another example of how K brings about a shift of their roles within the studio working process.

Participants are (in alphabetical order) as follows. K = Karen. S = Sophie. For transcription conventions, see the Appendix.

Figure 9: Karen finished her version and asks Sophie if she wants to try it. Karen's studio, Hackney Wick (08/2013) (Image: AM).

Do you want to *try* it? (extract)   31 seconds

---

01 K: *that she .. is dead*

02 S: *that her heart has stopped* . no that was really good .

---

03 K: I know it still does not give that much information . but it does . it does deal

04 S: no it did

---

05 K: with communism   yeah yeah yeah

06 S: it did create a very . yeah yeah yeah . I think I think u:h.

---

07 K: that kind of works so do you want to try it? .

08 S: that was really really good .   yeah

---

09 K: ((K passes S piece of paper)) try it ((humorously in a different voice)) (???

10 S: oh Lord . Karen

---

11 K: ???)+   I think you'd stand up though

12 S: ((a bit reluctant and not impressed)) I know . I am just

---

13 K: go to the other side of the room . . go ((in a different voice)) *do it as a*

---

14 K: *puppet show* .*do it as a little puppet show*

K has finished her turn of working on performing a section of the script (in line 01: *that she .. is dead*). S is engaged, provides an alternative ending of the scripted text (in line 02: *that her heart has stopped*) and immediately gives K her feedback which is very positive. K is at first self-critical about her performing the script (in lines 03 and 05), states that the way she performed it might work (in line 07: *that kind of works*) and then, without any hesitation, moves on to ask S if she wants to try it (in line 07: *do you want to try it?*). S seems rather surprised by being asked if she would like to try it (in line 10: *oh Lord . Karen*) and is not impressed by having to abandon her role of a spectator and swap it for the role of the performer. K tries to cheer her up in a humorous way (in lines 13 and 14: *do it as a little puppet show*) and supports her by giving S some ideas of how to start (in lines 11 and 13).

4. The artist's voice and shift of roles in Control Signal

In the artistic production process of *Control Signal*, the two collaborators jointly created a script and worked on oralizing it. In the interactive situation of performance arts/drama production processes, one can usually find different examples of multivoicedness as collaborators will adopt different voices and shift back and forth between multiple voices. We have looked at three types of voices adopted by the performers. (1) Throughout the working process, they carried out various communicative activities, such as talking about what the text is supposed to convey and how it is supposed to be performed. (2) They also carried out dramatized versions (acting versions) of parts of the text through manner of speaking, prosody and so on, to express their suggestions. (3) The third voice that was identified (in example 1) is the artistic practitioner's voice (following the Bakhtinian idea that voice incorporates an element of perspective; Bakhtin 1984).

The shifting of roles, initiated by K, seems to help maintain a flow, a playfulness and a balance of responsibility and power, so that the roles of the two collaborators are never set but are shaken up. Involvement and decision-making in the collaborative working process need to be constantly negotiated, tried out and stimulated. As we have seen, discussing the aim of a role-shift could bring about engagement and playfulness (in example 1, when S says in a humorous way that she could have said anything to K), or, as in example 2, a role-shift can challenge another performer, who in this case seems to have settled into the role of spectator.

The initiation of shifting of roles can be identified as an important feature in the studio working process of *Control Signal* and of K's artistic practice within this production. It creates a challenge for the collaborators, facilitating flow and ensuring that roles are not set, and promotes playfulness, and in this production, where the two performers differ in a number of ways (e.g. experience in devising work and performing it, language, age and knowledge of other cultures), the shifting of roles has the function of creating a more equal working relationship between them.

References

Bakhtin, Mikhail (1984), *Problems of Dostoevsky's Poetics* (trans. C. Emerson), Minneapolis and London: University of Minnesota.

Cameron, Deborah (2001), *Working With Spoken Discourse*, London: Sage.

Ehlich, Konrad and Rehbein, Jochen (1976), 'Halbinterpretative Arbeitstranskriptionen (HIAT)', *Linguistische Berichte*, 45, pp. 21–41.

Grésillon, Almuth (1999), *Literarische Handschriften: Einführung in die 'critique génétique'*, Bern: Lang.

Levinson, Stephen (1992), 'Activity types and language', in P. Drew and J. Heritage (eds), *Talk at Work*, Cambridge: Cambridge University Press, pp. 66–100.

Milde, Andrea (2007a), 'Directing: A Collaborative Artistic Task-Oriented Spoken Communication Process', *The International Journal of the Arts in Society*, 1:5, pp. 25–30.

Milde, Andrea (2007b), 'Multivoicedness and artistic reformulations in directing-conversations', in R. Weinert (ed.), *Spoken Language Pragmatics: An Analysis of Form-Function Relations*, London: Continuum, pp. 182–207.

Milde, Andrea (2007c), 'Art as a Process of Revision: The Audience and the End Product', *The International Journal of the Arts in Society*, 2:2, pp. 151–56.

Milde, Andrea (2012), 'Spoken language and doing drama', Urban Language and Literacies Working Paper series, WP89, King's College London, https://www.academia.edu/6351219/WP89_Milde_2012._Spoken_language_and_doing_drama. Accessed 31 December 2020.

Milde, Andrea (2019), 'Linguistics in drama processes', Urban Language and Literacies Working Paper series, WP251, King's College London, https://www.academia.edu/39625216/WP251_Milde_2019._Linguistics_in_drama_processes. Accessed 31 December 2020.

Milde, Andrea, Christopher, Karen and Grodin, Sophie (2014), '*Control Signal*: Different perspectives on the working process', keynote presentation at the symposium *Of Two Minds: An Afternoon on Duet Collaborations*, Drama, Theatre and Performance Department, University of Roehampton, Sadler's Wells, London, 30 October.

Schegloff, Emanuel, Jefferson, Gail and Sacks, Harvey (1977), 'The preference for self-correction in the organisation of repair in conversation', *Language*, 53, pp. 361–82.

Transcription conventions

Standard orthography is generally used here for the transcriptions with the following exemptions:

- punctuation marks are not used apart from apostrophes, question marks and exclamation marks;

- special features in articulation are demonstrated through untypical orthography.

((laughs))	double parentheses in smaller font represent comments for the following text.
+	plus sign indicates that comment in double parentheses stops working.
a:nd	colon stretches previous sound.
NO	capital letters in utterance elements indicate emphasis.
[...]	ellipses in brackets indicate places where the transcription has been abridged.
(??)	parentheses with one or more question marks indicate unintelligible words.
't'	apostrophe indicates non-verbal phenomena.
ok . so	each dot represents a pause with approximate length of one second.

---

but no	utterance elements written underneath in the system are spoken at the same time.

Introductory Fragment 3: Tangled

KAREN CHRISTOPHER

I wanted to be tangled with people. I did not want anyone to escape. If I involved them in a project, we might become entangled, and I wanted that. Of course until you become entangled, it is hard to know if that is what you want. Entanglement causes change, and some are uncomfortable with it. The change part. The infection. But not every infection is bad. I like the take-over feeling and a persuasive reason to get along. Entangling means other people or creatures or materials or subjects or states of being take up space in my head. This leads to the feeling that the entangled are somehow always with me.

I want to describe it along the lines of a sea creature, possibly like a squid or an octopus, whose long and independently intelligent tentacles wrap around and gain information, see or understand through various senses of proximity and touch and send information through the space between us with odour or colour or rhythm or vibration. Like you do above water but in the sea instead. I was at a funeral for my father-in-law who had always lived in the same small town and who had known and become entangled with many people, mostly through work but also through a lifetime of school and family and the social clubs he liked to invent. He was a tangler. At his funeral, I was positioned at the door with his son to greet those people attending the funeral on their way in. Each person looking into my eyes and holding my hand imprinted in such a way that I felt them lingering later for hours, for more than a day, for more than a week. And then I read about octopuses and recognized the feeling of arms everywhere surrounding me in the days following that funeral in that community where everyone knows their connection to everyone else.

The arms of the octopus came back to me; they slid back into my head and shook hands with the funeral mourners still lingering there.

Some days are so dark we keep all of the lights on. Some days the clouds process all the way along the sea to cuddle the mountains. Some days the bread dough would not let go and its tendrils cling to our fingers. Some days we shake the hand of every single person. This changes us forever; now we can always feel their arms like octopus tentacles around us. Some days the men shovel in the soil with urgency as if it does not matter their friend is down there or as if that is all that does. A fluid reality, this world is never the same. This oceanic world, everyone sending out tendrils, hanging on to one another. We do not fuse, we interweave, we resist the current, otherwise we are swept apart.

All around me I hear, I feel, tensions like vines wrapping around me, and my mother reaches through the night from another continent and her message gets through and mine back to her; she says,

Thoughts inside your head are mingled with everything you know and it's only when you have to say them out loud that they have to stand on their own or find that they are yet incomplete or in fact mean nothing outside your head. Sometimes the expression of them completes them as you speak and arrive as a surprise. Like a performance which has to take place in order to make its sense.

For years I worked closely with groups of people, and this work meant I carried those people tangled within my mind. At the end of a long series of complicated entanglements, I decided to work for a while with only one person at a time on only one project at a time. This prospect was more anxiety provoking than the groups I had been in before. Entanglement with only one person felt like an opportunity for deeper and possibly more troubling entanglement with less autonomy and an intimacy with a language all its own.

Imagining Seven Falls

MARY PATERSON

There are some things you will never know.

You will never know how it feels to wake up in someone else's body: to shrug on her skin and walk arm-in-arm with yourself towards the horizon. You will never know how it feels to be a stranger, watching as you speak into a loudhailer. You will never know the last words someone says to you, when you've already gone. You will never know if this moment is destined to become a significant one: the apparition of a boat from a thick, wet fog; a young musician's first paid gig; a flag unfurling from a far-off window.

During *Seven Falls*, two performers recite lines from a health and safety manual through loudhailers, into a strong wind. They are wearing identical red dresses and heavy, black shoes. They are standing outside, next to a body of water, and the guidance they are reading is for the context of water safety. It is a surreal scene. The setting, the equipment and the formal sounding language all suggest an official purpose. But the red dresses are not utilitarian enough to be uniforms, the women's voices struggle to be heard above the wind, and there is something rebellious in their gaze, staring straight ahead at an invisible horizon.

All this uncertainty is what the discipline of health and safety is for. Its language is designed to articulate things you will never know. It is good practice, in this context, to imagine a range of possible scenarios, so you can describe what to do next. Imagine you are trying to lift a submerged body. Imagine you are trying to lift a submerged body into a canoe. Imagine you are trying to hold onto another body – like your own, but with different skin; a different body but close in age and with many shared memories.

Imagine for a moment that you are me.

I am imagining a performance called *Seven Falls* by Teresa Brayshaw and Karen Christopher. I am imagining a performance that I have never seen, but which I have heard about in all the normal ways – in photographs, in film, in conversation. By listening to these forms of partial witness, I am constructing an imaginary memory of *Seven Falls*. In conversation, Teresa says she has an imaginary memory, too. She thinks of the photographs of each live show as part of the work. Sometimes, they capture what Karen calls 'emblematic moments', '[which] have to do with a configuration of bodies, and space, and the space that they're in'.

You will never know what really happened in the space of the past. You will never know what else was happening. You will never know what the stranger was thinking, his glance caught in the centre of the lens, as he walked behind something he was not expecting to see. (Or if you do, he will no longer be a stranger.) You will never know how it feels to lie in water as the last gulp of air leaves your lungs. (Or if you do, you won't remember.)

You will never know bone-shaking cold like it: the sensation of being submerged in ice cold water on an ice-cold day.

Imagine what it feels like to stand, shoulders touching, in the crisp air, next to a body of water. Imagine it is Remembrance Sunday, a day for collective imagining. Later, Teresa and Karen will walk towards the horizon, arm in arm, red dresses dripping with water. And then (maybe it will be here, or maybe it will be somewhere else), the people who have been watching them will approach two water-logged canoes and dip their own hands in the water. They are checking to see if it is really cold.

'Did I just see what I thought I saw?' asks Karen, imagining what the audience must have been thinking.

Imagine a sharp shock hits the tips of your fingers. They start to tingle.

In a conversation about *Seven Falls*, Teresa refers to the boat as a coffin. 'I don't think of the boat as a coffin', says Karen, so Teresa explains that her father died when she was four and she was taken to see him, in his coffin. Teresa's son was still a child when she performed *Seven Falls*, and he performed alongside her. There is a photograph of her son watching her lie down in a canoe during the performance. When she saw it, Teresa imagined herself as a child, seeing her father lying down for the final time.

It can be like that, imagination. It can take you by surprise, take you to unexpected places. It can be risky.

Imagine that you don't know if the water is ice cold or if it has been heated up, secretly. Imagine you don't know if this is a boat or a coffin. Imagine you don't know whether the ribcages of the two women who have been submerged in ice cold water are fluttering with warming breath or with the kind of shock that will draw a fistful of water into their lungs.

During *Seven Falls*, two performers recite lines from a health and safety manual through loudhailers, into a strong wind. Later (or is it earlier?), they recite words from the shipping forecast – that mesmerizing ritual, broadcast each evening by the BBC. Tailored for sailors but heard by many more, the shipping forecast provides a daily update of the British Isles' surrounding waters. It is part of Britain's collective imagining; how we know we are all at sea. In the performance, Teresa and Karen weave with the language of the shipping forecast to describe their own journeys to get here:

'I'm from near Shannon. North-easterly 5 to 7, decreasing 4 in north later', says Teresa, into a loudhailer, on a cold day, next to a body of water.

'I've been travelling north east', says Karen, standing nearby, 'losing my identity'.

In Spain, where the shipping forecast would be unfamiliar (so Teresa and Karen imagined) to a local audience, they raised toasts instead. Here's to the breakfast man and his busy schedule! Here's to the boatman for his strength and courage! Here's to the wind!

What all the forms of language spoken in *Seven Falls* have in common is the space to imagine things you will never know. Imagine the worst-case scenario. Imagine gales becoming moderate, later. Imagine the crisp satisfaction of wine brought to your lips, kissing a seal on the ideas you've just spoken.

Imagine you are standing shoulder to shoulder on a cold day: a day set aside for imagining. You are watching two women in red dresses and workman-like shoes. They are speaking into loudhailers, or getting into water-logged canoes, or dancing slowly in time with each other. They are similar in age, similar in height, and occasionally, they glance over to each other with a gentle warmness, as if to check the other is ok.

'It is not the water that will kill you', says Karen in a conversation with Teresa and me, 'but the cold'. The reason most people drown, she explains, is not because they are trapped without air, but because the shock of cold water makes them gasp for breath, makes them draw a fistful of water into their lungs.

(Imagine.)

In the first show, in Gateshead, the water was so cold in the canoes in which Teresa and Karen submerged themselves, that Karen thought she might not be able to do the dance that followed. It was so cold, she says, that even after the show, when she was wrapped up warm and drinking whisky, 'I thought I would never be warm again'. And *that*, she says, 'is what I wanted!'

Imagine you are falling.

Imagine you are failing. Imagine you are dying. Imagine this is something like a death, on something like a stage. Imagine you are falling from grace, falling from time, falling from one part of your life to another – different, but close in age and with many shared memories.

Imagine this is a different type of risk assessment.

Imagine a series of real risks. Teresa and Karen really step into real ice-cold water. They really submerge themselves until their skin is soaked with ice-cold water, really lie back until their hair coils like snakes in ice-cold water.

I have never seen *Seven Falls*, but I have spent a day talking to Teresa and Karen about it. The conversation was about the performance, but it was also a performance of its own – of the relationship between Teresa and Karen, developed over years of phone calls, studio time, conversation, sharing, jokes, laughter and a series of risks as real as the ones seen in public. 'We'll pull on several silk threads at once', wrote Karen in an email to Teresa, by way of an invitation; '... some of the details won't be immediately clear. For now it will be enough to know if you might like to join me'.

In this relationship, uncertainty was sewn in from the start, or rather, unravelled there.

And the process could not fail.

'This cannot fail' was a maxim that Teresa and Karen said aloud to each other during their years working together. It is both an imperative – *this must not fail!* – and a form of acceptance – *no-one can tell us this is a failure.* Or, as Teresa says, 'even when it doesn't feel great, it's important. The fact that it's not complete, beautiful or even satisfactory in some ways, is really important'.

This is where the risk comes in.

Despite the promises of language, or costume, or ritual, the processes of managing risk do not make it go away. The processes of anticipating, articulating or even poeticizing risk do not make it go away. They simply stop the risk being a stranger. A stranger to yourself or to other people. A stranger like the one I have seen captured in the middle of a photograph of *Seven Falls*, who is staring in surprise at the backs of Teresa Brayshaw and Karen Christopher, who are wearing red dresses and black shoes and speaking words from the shipping forecast into loudhailers on an ice-cold day.

... There are warnings of gales ...

... Occasionally very poor ...

Teresa says working closely with Karen was a way of 'encountering a "not-me"'. She and Karen are two women similar in age and height, from opposite sides of the world, and who have been on different journeys to get here. Meeting this 'not-me', says Teresa, meant that her own 'me' could be more apparent. 'Suddenly, I realize that who I am and how I operate is not only OK, it's absolutely welcomed'.

Would the stranger have been so surprised if two teenagers, or two women in their twenties, or two men of any age, were dressed up and performing like this in public? I do not imagine so. For women, being seen invariably means being seen *as*. Being seen as bossy, being seen as mild, being seen as attractive, or not attractive, useful or un-useful, young or old, parent, teacher, daughter ...

You might not know how it feels to be free of other people's expectations.

You might not imagine that kind of freedom could arise through a process of performing in public.

It's a risk.

'It's about trying to keep your head above water', Teresa says, about *Seven Falls*. 'It's about two women, in the middle of their lives, trying to keep their heads above water'.

The new version of Teresa that emerged in the process of the duet was in fact 'a version of "not-me"'. Herself, but different; close in age, with many shared memories, but without the limits of other people's expectations. Karen says the relationship that arose between the two of them *is* the work of art. And this, of course, is the reason it cannot fail. 'If it's about the piece, if it's about the thing between us, then my weakness, your weakness ... who the hell cares?'

Each of the women is bursting with energy. Imagine. Their energy seems connected to this work they are doing together, and also to be derived entirely from themselves.

Imagine you are not falling.

Teresa and Karen tell a story of how one detail got into the show. They were sharing a room before the performance in Bilbao, and Karen was reading while Teresa slept. She read about a species of moths that drinks the tears of sleeping birds, and she wanted to add a line about this to the script. The next morning, she waited. She waited until she and Teresa were walking along the curves of a river, and then, she tried it out.

'Silence ...' (says Karen, remembering Teresa's reaction), 'silence ... silence ... and then Teresa looks at me and says, "But Karen. *Why* are the birds crying?"'

You will never know exactly what someone else is thinking. You will never crouch inside her mind, watch her thoughts fire like electric sparks and catch them with a sharp shock in the tips of your fingers.

You will never know exactly which turn of phrase will be important to someone else. But you will know when she lets out a joyous, roaring laugh.

Imagine you are in a room with two performers – Teresa Brayshaw and Karen Christopher – and they are both roaring with laughter.

'I said in my mind', Karen recounts, gleefully, '"there's my girl ... it's all the way inside! It's inside the brain of Teresa Brayshaw!"'

Imagine you are trying to lift a body.

Imagine you are trying to keep a head above water.

Imagine it is your own head.

Imagine two people who are most themselves by virtue of being versions of not-themselves. By reaching towards each other, they realize their own limits. They balance on the brink of losing themselves, and they find their balance.

The meaning of this performance by Teresa and Karen (not just *Seven Falls*, but also the relationship that made it happen) arises from its hair's breadth distance from the impossible. This risk is not just manifest in the movements of Teresa and Karen and what emerges in between but also in the eyes and minds of audience members: witnesses to the near-impossible, conspirators in a collective imagining. 'Nothing we do', says Karen, 'has to be understood in only one way'. As she speaks, she starts to imagine again what an audience might be thinking, shoulders touching, on a day for imagining. 'You probably can't hear everything we're saying. So what you're really looking at is people struggling against the rain and the wind and their clothing'.

Imagine you can't quite hear the words these women are saying. Imagine the words are dancing on the wind. Imagine the words coil themselves in your hair and make an unfamiliar noise against your ear, like the sound of water, rising.

There are some things you will never know.

But there are no limits to your imagination.

In Cardiff, Teresa and Karen turn to face the water and wave at passing boats, just as they always do at a certain point in the show. A sailing boat glides into view, with the word COURAGE emblazoned on its side.

Imagine this is a different type of risk assessment.

The apparition of the boat is one of the emblematic moments Karen has described. The waving was planned, but the sailing boat was not – Teresa and Karen did not know that COURAGE would make itself known. But in a way, COURAGE was made possible by *Seven Falls* at that very moment. It was made possible by the frame of an emblematic moment, waving to the limits of our imaginations, risking a journey into the unknown.

Imagine.

Seven Falls is a performance made possible by what lies between two performers, animated by the attention of an audience that is willing to believe in risks.

Imagine.

You are trying to keep your head above water.

Imagine it is your own head.

Imagine you are me.

You are holding me.

I am holding in my imagination two women with their heads above water, a rebellious look in their eyes, and COURAGE on the horizon.

Introductory Fragment 4: A Lot of Rope

KAREN CHRISTOPHER

In *miles & miles*, one of the performance duets I made with Sophie Grodin, the two of us, tied to opposite ends of a 100 metre rope, move around a performance space for almost an hour before stopping to untangle the heap of rope between us. Somewhere between us, the rope goes through a pulley hanging from the ceiling. The combination of this fixed point in the middle, our separate trajectories through the space and the length of the rope between us meant a tangle occurred during every performance. It was inevitable. I became transfixed by questions: How did we untangle in front of you? How did we trust it was something to watch? Isn't it exasperating to watch two people untangling a knot? The untangling of a rope or string or other line or set of lines is a panic-inducing dilemma, why did we want to play it out in real, uncontrollable time in front of an audience?

The untangling is an unquestionable by-product of the forces and concerns we lay out in *miles & miles*. Something about the attempt at linearity or organization of a sense of life and its uncontrollability is at the heart of this performance work.

To organize a stream of consciousness unleashed into the world merely by being alive might well be an impossible task.

Undoing a knot is the kind of thing I dare not do in front of you. The pressure of another's gaze is unsettling to the mind of the untangler. It might be a job best performed alone; what might be streamlined for one person to sort out becomes precarious with two, each sees the knot or tangle from a different point of view. The binocular aspect is just enough to tip the apple cart. But, as we do work in tandem, we must exercise the capacity to refrain from turning on each other like over-heated rats in a crowded cage. We keep our nerve by knowing there is a future to survive together.

One day there will be a book about this, including, but not limited to, the following sections: taking the whole body through the loop, the performance of confidence and optimism, the technical terms we feigned to make it seem we were in control and the vicarious thrill, for the audience, of our ultimate victory. This last being made richer and more satisfying by a truly intransigent set of tangles. We never stopped untangling until we were completely untangled.

Seen out the corner of my eye, the metaphorical possibilities of untangling made it more interesting, but when I looked straight at it, they quished away like lemon pips. I am afraid to write about it, afraid that I cannot do it justice, that somehow I will only write a series of platitudes that amount to navel gazing. Also, there is a mystery to why people respond to something that, taken out of the performance – the context in which it had a chemical reaction – becomes inert and its formlessness no more than a joke explained.

There are two of us on this rope. When we walk, we drag our path behind us. We leave a trail, we bend, bight, loop and knot. Only later do we look back at the tangled web we wove.

Always on Uneven Ground

RAJNI SHAH

Everything falls into twos.
Even the things I try not to divide that way.

Linear, Non-linear.
Settler, Indigenous.
Dualistic, Non-dualistic.
Me, You.

Stories spin out from the edges of these pairings until the two points round back towards each other and become proximate enough to indicate a circle. Sometimes, they make jokes.[1]

Much as I try to access other modes, in the end, I often find that my thinking is painfully linear, dualistic, binary or rational. I stumble over my own pronouns, linguistic conditioning betraying plurality and the desire to be fluid.

But this time

        – in honour of a letter you once wrote to me, and in deep respect of the many Indigenous cultures that teach us over and over again how to be inside time completely differently –

I will write a spiral

, one that tries to come back around again and again to the same spot,

               knowing it will never be the same.

---

1. Eve Kosofsky Sedgwick, in her brilliant introduction to *Touching Feeling*, notes that '[e]ven to invoke *nondualism*, as plenty of Buddhist sutras point out, is to tumble right into a dualistic trap'. (Okay, so it's not exactly a joke. But it makes me laugh. There are other jokes too.) Eve Kosofsky Sedgwick (2002), *Touching Feeling: Affect, Pedagogy, Performativity*, Durham, NC: Duke University Press, p. 2.

Dear Karen, We used to meet, every week in some form, intended / in person / in absence. The whole thing was scheduled to be an hour and a half or a couple of hours. It was a time in which we got to drink tea together, chat, and do 'the practice', which involved sitting silently together, in an attempt to do nothing; Not meditative, nor proscriptive, it was to my mind and memory a kind of non-prescribed not-doing. It did not take a particular shape, except that we were both inside it, making an attempt, separately, side by side. Immediately following the not-doing, we would write. Not doing for x number of minutes, writing for x number of minutes. The formula of time varied with each meeting. We made it again and again and again and again. And the practice was one we returned to again and again. Again and again. I have a small notebook filled with the writings that emerged from these sittings over several long years.

The last time we met I wrote:

The quiet blue of your mouth hides behind those slow grey muscles. We have opened the building and everyone inside is holding perfectly still. You are poised to miss me, to miss us, to miss this. All that is required is to show up, to really just show up, to open our mouths and to exhale water. We have shied away from it too long, locked it away and abandoned it, and now there it is: light in the sky, muscles in our bodies, and our eyes burning quietly as they face each other. We have opened the building and everyone inside is holding perfectly still. The air between us is not wet or dry. Our hearts beat strangely in our bodies today. It is just like any day except that time is not being measured externally. Holding still, there is no time between us, only what is being held within. The blue, the deep blue, the unsung, the awkward, the unpopular. Spirals, the sound of grain being poured from one vessel to another, the feeling of being trusted and the feeling of being heard. Fish, berries, non-human tracks along the water. A doctor, a door that has been created to be the size of an average human, half of a building, the memory of light. The feeling of grain being poured from one vessel to another.

All that is required is to show up, to really just show up, to open our mouths and to exhale water.

We already knew that day was the end of something. We had decided it would be our last time. I was about to move to what I would come to learn was Gadigal land, one small part of the many lands presently known together as Australia. You were at that time intending to stay in London, though later you too would move away from there. The sensation of this final writing was pointed. Our practice was one that resisted the pointiness of time, and yet, there it was, seeping through as we wrestled with our watery emotions. We drank tea, did the practice, and said: see you soon. And indeed, a day or so later, you came round to my home and delivered a book to me, as if to say: we will always see each other soon.

But this writing was supposed to be about listening and the duet.

Instead, it has become about you and me.

When I think about duet, I think about the many people contained in each of us.

When I think about duet, I think about coloniality, and formal dancing.

When I think about duet, I think about intimacy.

When I think about listening, I think about gathering.

When I think about listening, I think about how we are all already heard and seen.

When I think about listening, I think about assumptions and backstories.

When I think about listening, I think about houses in the night.

Our hearts beat strangely in our bodies today.

Were there two of us in the room each time we met? Maybe. Sometimes we sat in cafes or other public places, sharing our silent companionship with city noisescapes, other conversations, people catching trains. Those noises would enter into the 'not-doing', dance with our memories and desires and leave some trace on the page. Every time, there were others, joining the parade of companions in our act of holding open. Sometimes we talked and drank tea before we sat, and those conversations, emotions, unspoken things, became our insistent companions as we sat.

What I am saying is that in order to practise doing nothing, we had to get really quiet. And whenever we got really quiet, other lives flooded in. So began the ghost work. First, we were inviting or barring those other voices: come in, join me, be part of my listening; please become a thought that passes through, I don't want to be stuck here holding on to you too tightly. Then, they became us, morphing into colours and objects inside rooms that we saw with our eyes shut. Later, we could not tell where our bodies ended and the world began. Perhaps this was the point of the duet, that our edges would become contaminated by the many worlds that blurred between us on those days. Or perhaps the duet was not ever happening between us but between our actions: maybe it was a duet between doing nothing and writing. Two quiet movements side by side. We, the vessels within which they became filled and emptied themselves.

I wanted the feeling of being trusted and the feeling of being heard.

There were so many blanks on the cards of my memory, and yours. When we met, we were always forgetting things: names, stories, anecdotes we had wanted to share with each other. Lately, I have come to notice that this forgetting plasters over other kinds of memories: hurts, confrontations, shames and near misses of those things. The holding open was a kind of amnesty for both the memory and the imagination. We were free during that time from having to explain why there were so many gaps. Later, in a different room, we would completely fail to listen to each other, our ears crowded out by fear and loss. This time, there was no amnesty, and we found ourselves having to confront the bluntness of our tools. Listening as patchy signals struggling through, covered over by the lies we told ourselves, filled with histories and geographies that were designed to obliterate curiosity and care.

When I think about listening, I think about how we are always on uneven ground.

We have shied away from it too long.

I suppose what I am saying is that making it two does not make it simple. If anything, it complicates things. Just when we think we have narrowed it down, determined the parameters, honed in on the detail, new worlds emerge. Within each layer of attentiveness lies a whole other world we had previously failed to notice. Within each listening lies plurality.

Or maybe what I am saying is that I believe duets are non-binary. Like all those things that turn out to be plural and complex, a duet turns out not to be about two at all, but about the multitudes of tiny planets spinning in each supposed body.

A duet is a way of paying attention. And attention always yields complexity.

The quiet of your mouth.

Our eyes burning quietly.

Everyone is between us.

TwoFold: Questions

MARY PATERSON

Who is missing?

How do you know?

What shape do they make with their absence?

Will you start again when they get here?

Will you feel complete?

Will you feel better?

What is your position?

Who is your opposite?

Who is your complement?

What does your reflection say back to you from the mirror?

Be honest: how long do you like to spend talking to yourself in the mirror?

And how long would you like to do it if no one was watching? And how long would you like to do it if you could guarantee that people were watching, avidly, in silence, and theorizing it later on in company as the performance of an alter ego?

What kind of moral license could you achieve from dividing up your psyche into the other versus the self, the organized versus the active, the repressed versus the carnivalesque, the curator versus the artist?

What authority do you have when you give yourself a job title?

Is 'collaborator' a job title? Is 'partner'? Is 'scientist'? Is 'dyad'?

Is it a compliment?

What is your word for it?

Relatively speaking: what is your position?

What is your super-position?

How do you know you are not missing any information?

How do you know you are not drowning in misunderstanding?

What kinds of freedoms could you achieve when you know that entanglement is not to do with ignorance but to do with randomness?

How do you know?

In this context, what is the difference between knowledge and belief? I mean, what is the difference between knowing about entanglement and believing it to be true?

What do you believe in, passionately?

What happens if I ask you to share it with me?

What happens if we make a commitment about it, like a mortgage, or a funding application, and so we write it down as a list, or an equation, or a diary entry, or a transcribed piece of pop culture, or a participatory exercise, or a universal class, or a contract, or a diagram, or a practice-based PhD, or a programme printed three months in advance, or an autobiographical theatre show, or a stage direction, or a score, or a video you show when she is not there, or an abstract, or a piece of quantum cryptography designed to harness the uncertainty principle in order to ensure the certainty of your government's private positions?

What has happened, then?

How quickly does it change?

Who is measuring?

Would you rather have perfect knowledge of your position and maximal uncertainty of your direction of travel, or perfect knowledge of your velocity, and absolutely no idea where you are?

What is the relationship between politics and collaboration?

What is your word for it?

Is it bitter or sweet? Happy or sad? Collaborative or competitive? Yours or mine? Ours or theirs? Us or them, or us instead of them? Is this working for you? Is this work? Or this? Or this? Or this? Is this working?

Do you believe in expertise?

Do you need something from me?

Do you think that being a patient and enthusiastic teacher is the best kind
of basis for a working partnership?

Would you prefer to be the teacher or the student?

In what circumstances might ignorance be bliss, misunderstanding be
a resource, irritation be a creative energy?

Are you Good Cop or Bad Cop?

Female or Non-female? Trained or Untrained?

In your comfort zone or dragged into someone else's?

Do you think that the person you are thinking of would describe you
as generous?

Do you miss this person when they are not there?

Have you formalized your working relationship?

Did you formalize it in advance or in retrospect?

Did formalizing it make it more palatable to other people or did it make it easier for
you to work together again, or neither, or both?

What kinds of moral and artistic freedoms could you achieve when you know that
entanglement is not to do with accident but to do with precedent?

What kinds of freedoms could you achieve even if you do not know this, but if you
make it look that way, in a format that is designed to be recognized by other people?

What is your word for it: this intimacy, this fragility, this entanglement, this
uncertainty, this thing that would not be measured, this metaphor, this sculpture,
this material process?

What is your word for it: this accident, this facility, this circumstance, this
happenstance, this competition between us, this irritation I feel, this appearance of
your name next to mine as if we do not rub each other up the wrong way?

How long did you spend talking to yourself in the mirror this morning?

Are you aware that it is impossible to see yourself?

No, I mean really: have you stopped to think about the reciprocity
of recognition?

And have you stopped to think that if recognition is reciprocal, if being
seen is a collaborative act, then does this mean that you could change your identity
simply by changing the people that are looking at you?

Who is measuring?

What is your position?

How would you write this down?

Is this about process or anecdote or the fragility of bodies?

Do you trust me to stay within two arms' lengths of your skin?

Do you trust me to sculpt the space for you before you put on your outfit and get ready
to be seen?

Are you certain?

Would you rather be inside the room with something strange, or would you prefer it if
I said I could guarantee to keep all the strangers outside?

How will you describe this period in your life, differently, in retrospect?

How much do I irritate you?

What irritates you the most?

What have you learnt?

What shape is left by the words of the things we will never say to each other, or never
say about each other, even in retrospect?

Do you draw that shape around you like a blanket, or does it scratch against your skin?

Is there a 'them' and an 'us'? And if so, are we an 'us' or are you always going to be 'one
of them'?

What if you made a point to be seen performing next to someone who looks very
different to you?

What if you made a point to be seen performing next to someone who looks kind of
the same, at least once a year, every year until one of you dies?

Would this mean you could embrace randomness, or would it mean that you were
trying to measure it?

Would this make you an expert, or a loner, or a person projecting her shadow onto the nearest strange thing?

Do you have a word for it: this feeling; this position?

Have you realized how much you have changed? Have you thought about our shared vision recently? Is it revolutionary? Is it revolutionary yet? Is it an endless revolution? Have we abandoned our positions? Are we going to stay like this, forever, working on velocity?

Can you think of a less positive term than creative resistance?

Are you using your own words or is this some kind of joint strategy?

Are you a foreigner here?

Have you been listening to my ideas? Can I compliment you, for a second?

Can I instrumentalize our friendship?

Can I protect our past selves from any of this?

Are you my professional indemnity insurance? Are you taking something from me?

Are you seeing other people?

Shall we exchange a series of half silences, because to do anything else would be to skin our friendship and roast it over someone else's fire?

Shall we walk through fire together?

Shall we tie our hair in knots?

Shall we think about our outfits?

Would you call it friendship, or collaboration, or solidarity?

Would you call it competition, or partnership, or professional development?

Are you certain?

Are you secure?

Are you needy?

Are you in the limelight, or in someone else's shadow?

Are you lonely?

Are you coping?

Are you my coping mechanism?

Are you willing to carry on regardless?

Are you seeing other people?

Is the feeling mutual?

This text was commissioned as part of the TwoFold festival of duet performances (2017).

Always Already: Material in Progress

When I made these photographs with Karen and Tara, the room was filled with thoughts about the mechanical, the hybrid of analogue and digital technology, plants growing in the human body and the accumulation of small acts. The architecture of the studio was a huge loom, and Karen and Tara were weaving in the space at different scales.

There was a type of video format going round on social media at the time – facsimiles of objects that, when sliced, are revealed to be cake. I was drawn to the idea of something looking like something else or feeling like something it is not made of. So, the idea of cloth as book page was appealing in that way.

– Jemima Yong

Always Already is an 8-hour performance installation by Karen Christopher and Tara Fatehi Irani, which uses materials, text, sound and movement to explore the weaving together of plant, human and machine. We are making a machine that assembles the performance – a machine constructed of 100 forgotten questions. *Always Already* is rooted in the time and duration of work and gently connects histories of technological development with human touch. How does a repeated small gesture change the world? The two performers are women, working, of different ages, different origins, different languages – they connect, and have connected, and are interwoven.

Jemima Yong was invited to do a photo session with the two of us and the material we were working with not only because we needed something to represent the performance in advance of its completion but also because we were hoping to see something we would not otherwise see and understand something new about what we were doing.

my heart was found
displaced to the left,

my death revealed
an invasion of lace,
in both ventricles of the lung
a thick velvet having lined my stomach

only the appearance
of a circle of mushrooms
hinted at the fertile nature deep within
and a strong central trunk

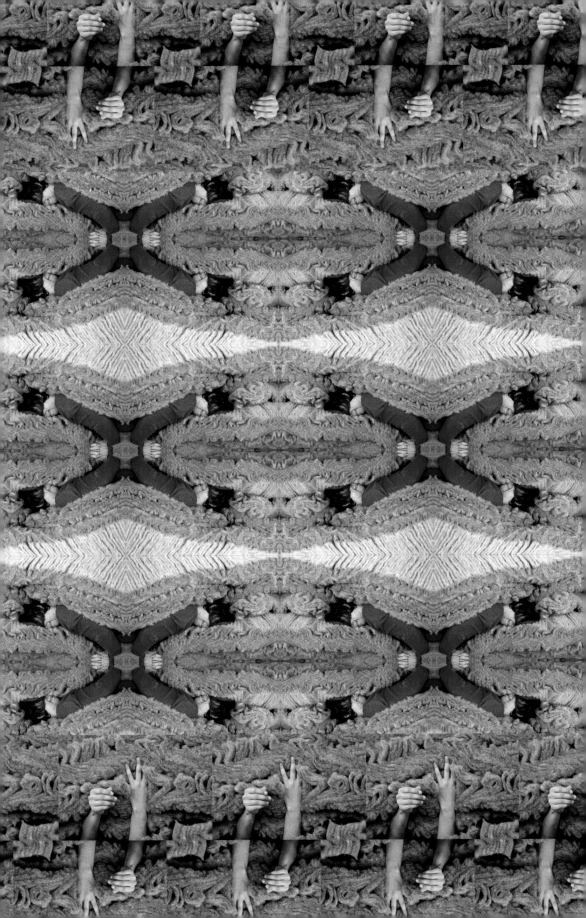

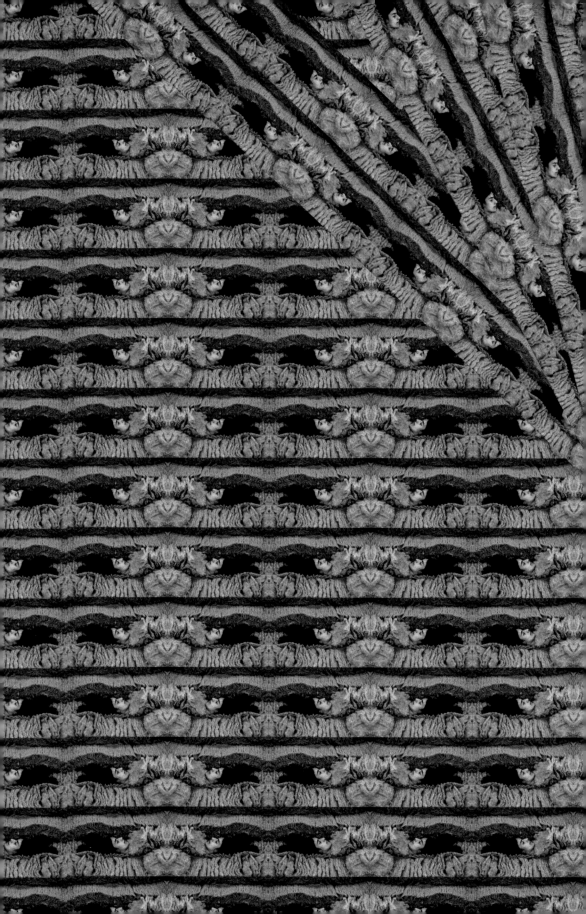

26. I inhaled some seeds as an experiment.
Will they grow inside me?

15. Last night I saw my lungs. Oh my....
Two monstrous piles of flesh with interlocking trees.
How do I forget?

86. The roots were breathing under my feet
and I didn't know where to stand,
not to suffocate the huge breathing roots,
going up and down at every breath.
And I thought how come I'm only seeing this now?

A Physics Duet

DAVID BERMAN

Bringing together different phenomenon and making seemingly different things emerge from a single point of view have always been the goal of physics.

This is the singular and central idea that has driven physics since Newton's time. *Unification* is the attempt to explain seemingly different phenomena by a single overarching concept. Perhaps the first example of this came from Newton himself, who, in his 1687 work *Principia Mathematicae*, explained that the motion of the planets in the solar system, the motion of the Moon around the Earth and the force that holds us to the Earth are all part of the same thing: the force of gravity. We take this for granted today, but pre-Newton, the connection between a falling apple and the orbit of the Moon would have been far from obvious and quite amazing.

The next key unifying discovery was made around 180 years after Newton by James Clerk Maxwell. Maxwell showed that electrostatics and magnetism are just different aspects of a single thing called electromagnetism. In the process, Maxwell discovered electromagnetic waves. These waves are in fact light – in bringing together and unifying, Maxwell had inadvertently explained light.

Another 200 years on, in 1984, the unification story continues. Abdus Salam and Steven Weinberg showed that the electromagnetic force and the weak nuclear force, which causes radioactive decay, are both just different aspects of a single force called the electroweak force.

This leaves us with three fundamental forces of nature: gravity, the electroweak force and the strong nuclear force that holds protons together.

Unifying matter

That deals with the forces, but what about matter? Many ancient belief systems have postulated that matter – and reality itself – is made from a finite number of elements. Modern physics confirms this idea. Experiments performed with the particle accelerator at CERN in Geneva have shown that there are just twelve basic building blocks of matter. These are known as the *elementary particles*. Everything we have ever seen in any experiment, here or in distant stars, is made of just these twelve elementary particles. All this is truly impressive: the entire Universe, its matter and its dynamics explained by just three forces and twelve elementary objects. It is good, but we would like to do better, and this is where string theory first enters: it is an attempt to unify further. To understand this, we have to tell another story.

Quantum gravity: an impossible marriage

There have been two great breakthroughs in twentieth-century physics. These two ideas provide the dramatis personae for the physics of the twenty-first century.

The first and perhaps the most famous is Einstein's theory of general relativity. The other equally impressive theory is quantum mechanics.

General relativity is itself a unification. Einstein realized that space and time are just different aspects of a single object he called *spacetime*. Massive bodies like planets can warp and distort spacetime, and gravity, which we experience as an attractive force, is in fact a consequence of this warping. Just as a pool ball placed on a trampoline will create a dip that a nearby marble will roll into, so does a massive body like a planet distort space, causing nearby objects to be attracted to it.

The predictions made by general relativity are remarkably accurate. In fact, most of us will have inadvertently taken part in an experiment that tests general relativity: if it were false, then global positioning systems would be wrong by about 50 metres per day. The fact that GPSs work to within five metres in ten years shows just how accurate general relativity is.

The second great breakthrough of the twentieth century was quantum mechanics. One of the key ideas here is that the smaller the scale at which you look at the world, the more random things become. *Heisenberg's uncertainty principle* is perhaps the most famous example of this. The principle states that when you consider a moving particle – for example, an electron orbiting the nucleus of an atom – you can never ever measure both its position and its momentum as accurately as you like. Looking at space at a minuscule scale may allow you to measure the position with a lot of accuracy, but there will not be much you can say about momentum. This is not because your measuring instruments are imprecise. There simply is not a 'true' value of momentum but a whole range of values that the momentum can take, each with a certain probability. In short, there is randomness. This randomness appears when we look at particles at a small enough scale. The smaller one looks, the more random things become!

The idea that randomness is part of the very fabric of nature was revolutionary: it had previously been taken for granted that the laws of physics did not depend on the size of things. But in quantum mechanics, they do. The scale of things does matter, and the smaller the scale at which you look at nature, the more different from our everyday view of the world it becomes: randomness dominates the small-scale world.

Again, this theory has performed very well in experiments. Technological gadgets that have emerged from quantum theory include the laser and the microchip that populate every computer, mobile phone and MP3 player.

But what happens if we combine quantum mechanics and relativity? According to relativity, spacetime is something that can stretch and bend. Quantum mechanics says that on small scales, things get random. Putting these two ideas together implies that on very small scales, spacetime itself becomes random, pulling and stretching, until it eventually pulls itself apart.

Evidently, as spacetime is here and this has not happened, there must be something wrong with combining relativity and quantum mechanics. But what? Both these theories are well tested and believed to be true.

How do we combine two ideas whose union leads to self-contradiction? How can the two be made to dance to one tune?

Physics often proceeds by finding a hidden assumption. It seeks the things we take for granted as true that need not be. Often, these are ideas that are so deeply ingrained that we never notice or question them. Progress is when we find these assumptions, question them and then throw them out.

There is an assumption that it is possible to consider smaller and smaller distances and get to the near infinitesimal point where spacetime pulls itself apart. What has rested in the back of our minds is that the basic indivisible building blocks of nature are point-like – but this may not necessarily be true.

Strings to the rescue

This is where string theory comes to the rescue. It suggests that there is a smallest scale at which we can look at the world: we can go that small but no smaller. String theory asserts that the fundamental building blocks of nature are not like points but like strings: they have extension – in other words, they have length. And that length dictates the smallest scale at which we can see the world.

What possible advantage could this have? The answer is that strings can vibrate. In fact, they can vibrate in an infinite number of different ways. This is a natural idea in music. We do not think that every single sound in a piece of music is produced by a different instrument; we know that a rich and varied set of sounds can be produced by even just a single violin. String theory is based on the same idea. The different particles and forces are just the fundamental strings vibrating in a multitude of different ways.

The mathematics behind string theory is long and complicated, but it has been worked out in detail. But has anyone ever seen such strings? The honest answer is 'no'. The current estimate of the size of these strings is about 10^{-34} metres, far smaller than we can see today, even at CERN. Still, string theory is so far the only known way to combine gravity and quantum mechanics, and its mathematical elegance is for many scientists a sufficient reason to keep pursuing it.

The theory's predictions

If string theory is indeed an accurate model of spacetime, then what else does it tell us about the world?

One of its more startling and most significant predictions is that spacetime is not four- but ten-dimensional. It is only in ten dimensions of spacetime that string theory works. So where are those six extra dimensions? The idea of hidden dimensions was in fact put forward many years before the advent of string theory by Theodor Kaluza and Oskar Klein.

Shortly after Einstein described the bending of space in general relativity, Kaluza and Klein considered what would happen if a spatial dimension would bend round and rejoin itself to form a circle. The size of that circle could be very small, perhaps so small that it could not be seen. Those dimensions could then be hidden from view. Kaluza and Klein did show that in spite of this, these dimensions could still have an effect on the world we perceive. Electromagnetism becomes a consequence of the hidden circle with motion in the hidden dimension being electric charge. Hidden dimensions are possible, and they in fact can give rise to forces in the dimensions that we can see.

String theory has embraced the Kaluza–Klein idea, and currently, various experiments are being devised to try and observe the hidden dimensions. One hope is that the extra dimensions may have left an imprint on the *cosmic microwave background*, the leftover radiation from the Big Bang, and that a detailed study of this radiation may reveal them. Other experiments are more direct. The force of gravity depends crucially on the number of dimensions; so, by studying gravitational forces at short distances, one can hope to detect deviations from Newton's law and again see the presence of extra dimensions.

Mathematics and physics have always influenced each other, with new mathematics being invented to describe nature and old mathematics turning out to lend perfect descriptions for newly discovered physical phenomena. String theory is no different, and many mathematicians work on ideas inspired by it. These include the possible geometries of the hidden dimensions, the basic ideas of geometry when there is a minimum distance, the ways in which strings can split and come together and the question of how we can relate strings to the particles in the world that we see.

String theory gives us an exciting vision of nature as miniscule bits of vibrating string in a space with hidden curled-up dimensions. All the implications of these ideas are yet to be understood. String theory is an active area of research with hundreds of people working to see how the theory fits together and produces the world we see around us.

The story

We began bringing together opposing ideas. There was an obstruction, an impasse, and for years, science was held back. Then we went and found the assumptions we held on to that were never consciously made. After rejecting those deeply held ideas, we could unify and in doing so found a new way of seeing the world...

Conclusion: I Have Been Thinking of You This Whole Time

MARY PATERSON

And what about you?

How are you? if that is not an empty question. It often *is* an empty question, but I promise I am going to listen.

No, really. I ask, 'how are you?' and I really want to know. I want to know how your heart felt when you woke up this morning, which large and small griefs are held behind your eyes like an unripe tear, which anticipations are burning just below your skin.

Sometimes, I think there are too many words in the world. Too many words, saying too many things. Take these, for example. But then I remember that words are not spoken or written down in order to prevent more words from happening. Quite the opposite.

I once attended a lecture series given by a man who read passages from his recently published book on the subject. 'Some people are surprised that I am reading from my own book', he explained, a few weeks in. 'But I have nothing else to say'. I do not think people were surprised about the book but that he was willing to transpose the words from page to stage without any introduction, conclusion or other forms of translation. It was as if he did not realize we were there, or perhaps he did not care. There is a reason why an essay (for example) tends to be written in a different way to a play: because it finds its audience in a different kind of situation. For the same reason, the way you talk to 100 people is not the same as the way you might talk to one.

Quite the opposite.

Words are uttered, muttered, sighed and screamed in order for more words to happen. It is a type of care, of taking care.

And what about you?

This book is about duets. Not duos, as Karen Christopher points out in these pages, but an *other* form that is produced when two people work together. This careful distinction in language is important because the duet is a third element, like the Tartini tone that emerges between two notes, or the rainbow that emerges between sun and rain, or the meaning that emerges between what one person says (writes/ speaks/gestures) and what another person comes to understand (read/listen/ watch). A duet is a creation, both more real and less real than the elements that made it possible.

A rainbow, for example, is made up of droplets of water and light, and nothing more. But a rainbow is not just water and light. It is also a rainbow.

This has two obvious consequences. First, a duet is an action sustained by both partners. In the Jewish tradition, as Orit Kent describes, students of Talmudic texts often work in partnership to read, question and analyse the holy scriptures. This practice, named *havruta* (literally 'partnership' or 'companionship'), places two students together on an equal plain. Nobody is the teacher. Nobody is in charge. Nobody has an answer, and having an answer is not the point anyway. The students form a relationship with the text through their relationship with each other. Their understanding of their faith is explored through the practice of this dynamic: a slow dance between two minds.

Second, a duet can trace the shape of its own origin story. As J. R. Carpenter writes, it is frequently clear, whether you are standing on the edge of a jagged coastline or on the borders of an unanswerable question, that '[t]here aren't two of something, but there *should* be' (original emphasis). Without one or more of its duo partners, a duet can be a type of loss. Carpenter writes about castaway literature – words and ideas fermented in the days of European colonialism, when a few men's imaginary landscapes carved the globe so brutally that most people were left stranded. But I am also thinking of earlier colonialists. The oldest word in the Danish language is a Viking word for 'longing'. I like to imagine groups of blood thirsty, eighth-century warriors, camped together on strange rocks, looking out to sea and longing for home.

This presents a paradox. If a duet is both a practice sustained by two elements and the shape those elements leave behind, then is it moving or still, alive or dead, evolving or complete?

The answer is yes.

There is a paradox of writing, too. Writing is done for you, the reader, when you are not yet there. By the time you have arrived, the writing is finished – complete – and you are invited to receive it, whole, like a pill. This is true. And it is not true, as you know if you have ever read something more than once. The meaning that emerges from a book you last read five, ten, 50 years ago is nothing like the meaning that emerged that first time.

Quite the opposite.

In both cases, the appearance of a paradox is actually the appearance of a hidden assumption. The hidden assumption is that meaning comes from a single mind: I think, therefore I am. But, as Donna Haraway explains in her book *Staying With the Trouble*, the Cartesian approach to individual thought (which, incidentally, arose in Europe at the height of its colonial endeavours) makes a fundamental mistake about the interdependence of every living thing. 'Nothing makes itself', Haraway says, 'nothing is really autopoietic or self-organizing' (2016: 53). For this reason, she describes living creatures as 'companion species', a category that 'helps me refuse human exceptionalism [...] The partners do not precede the knotting; species of all kinds are consequent upon worldly subject- and object-shaping entanglements' (13).

The story of a paradox revealing a hidden assumption is also the one that David Berman tells about physics, in its attempts to unify Einstein's theory of relativity with the randomness of quantum mechanics. It seems impossible that the world is predictable at a large scale (relativity) and unpredictable at a small scale (quantum mechanics). One solution to this is the concept of string theory, which suggests there are dimensions of experience we cannot perceive, describe or measure. String theory posits at least five dimensions that exist beyond our abilities to know them. We can only feel their consequences.

We are the coastlines singing to the other side of the ocean. We are the Vikings wishing for home. The ideas that hang like clouds between two students, the audience member sitting in the stalls, gazing at a body that moves on stage, thinking about love.

The Vikings used to put two words together to create a kenning – a kind of poetic description of another thing. The sea might be a whale-trail. Or a sail-trail. A ship was a wave-swain. Or a sea-stead. (Later, this became a form of Icelandic poetry.)

A duet might be a string-dimension, or a listen-speak, or a rain-bow.

This book is about duets, and it is rooted in a specific way of making duets: the performance practice of Karen Christopher. She has been making duets with her company, Haranczak/Navarre Performance Projects, since 2010. The company name is itself a duet, formed from the names of Christopher's two grandmothers. For native English speakers, Haranczak/Navarre reveals the dimensions of movement, migration, placement and displacement that are otherwise hidden in Karen Christopher's name. (Hidden, or concealed, because the hope of the ultimate duet form – the child – is that it might be free of the deprivations of its ancestors.)

For Christopher, the duet is a form of responsibility. Having worked in a larger group of performance makers for years, she embarked on a project that would explore the particular 'resonance' of two. This is what she and Sophie Grodin describe when they write, together, about the ecology of their working practices. One of Carpenter's questions is useful here: 'What if we ask not what is the action produced by two of something, but where?' Together, Christopher and Grodin describe the terrain of the duet as a kind of attentive longing for consensus. This does not mean that everyone must be kept happy, comfortable, afloat. (Quite the opposite.) It might mean destabilizing things, putting one person at a disadvantage, making her speak an unfamiliar language. In this way, the duo partners ensure equal access to a space in which the duet can arise.

It is a type of care. It is a type of taking care.

This responsibility has two obvious consequences. First, a duet generates its own forms of knowledge. The careful attention that Andrea Milde gives to the language used by Christopher and Grodin in the rehearsal room, for example, generates a map of their relationship: the duet of their speech acts, as they project versions of themselves into a middle space where they can meet. Similarly, when Litó Walkey recalls her duets with other performers, she is writing a score for their encounters at the same time as she is encountering them again in her imagination. ('Imagination', writes the poet Etel Adnan, creates 'both the windows and what we see' [2018: 32].)

Second, a duet is its own form of research. There are many ways of saying this, but none as succinctly as the words used by Rajni Shah. 'A duet is a way of paying attention. And attention always yields complexity'.

This time, there is no paradox. To be responsible to another person is to pay attention to them. To pay attention to something is to be attuned to its greater complexity. Moving or still, alive or dead, evolving or complete.

(Yes.)

And so, when Teresa Brayshaw describes working with Karen Christopher, she talks of an encounter with a 'not-me'. This not-me allows her to be more fully herself, partly because of the differences she can perceive and partly because the differences open up a space in which she might discover something new. The not-me is a type of companion, just as it is for Jewish scholars, that challenges the (idea of the) individual without competing with them.

And so, when Eirini Kartsaki pays attention to performances by Haranczak/Navarre Performance Projects (among others), she thinks about her family, her lovers, her body, all the particles in it trembling in ways that are unmeasurable but that have profound consequences. Like physicists who desire unity and so discover new dimensions, this movement is a form of solidarity: '[i]t explores living and being with the other through wonder and curiosity'.

And so.

What about you?

Read-writing
Hide-finding
Meaning-making
Subject-shaping
Image-thinking
Double-taking

How are you?

It might seem like an empty question, but I promise I am going to listen. Well, we both know that's not quite how this will work, but indulge me. I am imagining you. I have been thinking of you this whole time.

A rainbow is made up of water and light, and nothing more. Nothing more but someone to see it. And when you see it, you do not see water and light. You see a rainbow.

This book is rooted in a specific performance practice, but the more that its two editors – Karen Christopher and Mary Paterson – paid attention to that practice, the wider we were encouraged to look for duets elsewhere: in scholarship, in science, in literature, in linguistics. The duet is both a material condition and a metaphor that makes the material possible. For this reason, none of the duets explored in this book have beginnings or endings.

'We have to agree', writes Christopher, 'when to stop making and start sharing the work'. She is referring to her performance practice, which is eventually released from a studio and placed in front of other people. At this point, the work becomes one element in a new duet, the audience the other, and the experience of the piece is the Tartini tone.

There are a number of pieces here that I (Mary Paterson) wrote in response to performances by Haranczak/Navarre Performance Projects, which I saw over a period of years. As I watched, I developed relationships with each performance, quivering, boiling, shivering, tangling. The writing is not a record of what I saw but of these relationships. And these relationships do not have beginnings or endings, either. Instead, they mutate into other forms of attention, which is where *you* come in.

Thoughts are uttered, muttered, sighed and screamed in order for more thoughts to happen.

Let us agree that this book is released, now, from its making and placed in front of you. At this point, the words written down become one element in a new duet. You are the other.

Meaning is both more real and less real than the elements that made it possible.

References

Adnan, Etel (2018), *Surge*, New York: Nightboat Books.

Haraway, Donna (2016), *Staying With the Trouble: Making Kin in the Chthulucene*, Durham, NC: Duke University Press.

Diffractions: Record of a Passage

DAVID WILLIAMS

In her writings and interviews, Donna Haraway has sometimes used the optical metaphor of diffraction to propose another way of looking at and thinking about things. She describes the physical process of diffraction as follows:

> when light passes through slits, the light rays that pass through are broken up. And if you have a screen at one end to register what happens, what you get is a record of the passage of the light rays onto the screen. This 'record' shows the history of their passage through the slits. So what you get is not a reflection; it's the record of a passage. (Haraway 2000: 103)

Haraway clarifies her deployment of this metaphor as a critical strategy:

> Diffraction patterns are about a heterogeneous history, not originals. Unlike mirror reflections, diffractions do not displace the same elsewhere. Diffraction is a metaphor for another kind of critical consciousness at the end of this rather painful Christian millennium, one committed to making a difference and not to repeating the Sacred Image of the Same. I'm interested in the way diffraction patterns record the history of interaction, interference, reinforcement, difference. In this sense, 'diffraction' is a narrative, graphic, psychological, spiritual and political technology for making consequential meanings. (Haraway 2000: 101–02)

What follows are just some of the 'diffraction patterns' that flicker for me in the wake of passing through the materials in this fine, thoughtful collection, or them passing through me. Rather than the closure of a reflexive summation, these texts bring together fragments of the voices of certain others who have somehow showed up these past weeks to duet (with) me in my reading, thinking and listening around the work of Karen Christopher's Haranczak/Navarre Performance Projects, and 'duets' more broadly. Right now as I write, while the waves of the Covid-19 global pandemic spread ever wider, the open secrets of systemic injustice, intolerance, inequity and oppression – historical and actual – are being radically exposed and contested around the world. At such a dynamic time more than ever, it seems essential and timely to listen to others. In part, this gathering of voices seeks to honour something akin to what Rajni Shah in her own contribution here describes as 'the parade of companions in our act of holding open'. To ask quietly, what if we attend for a moment to the co-presence of her and him and them and that over there: where do their songs lead?

So, the following texts propose a drawing together of various constitutive filaments from the duets explored in this book that also leaves some trailing threads to blow where they will. Above all, these texts are offered here in their partiality and multiplicity as purposefully playful responses, their 'meanings' consequential or otherwise: quiet invitations, memories and associations, resonances and riffs, interferences, leaky displacements, dilations and detours along other related paths. Potential ways out, perhaps, opening into further possible engagements in the dynamic turbulence of the spaces between *two entangled somethings* – surely the most urgent choreography at every scale.

On waking up in the morning over these past weeks, I have often struggled to break free of the hold of my dreams, part of me still caught up in their whispering fronds and limbs, and I emerge into the day a little crumpled by their weight. This recurrent entanglement with the unconscious and its unresolved tensions in the mysterious night school of one's dreams, a duet many people seem to have experienced more regularly and vividly in recent times, seems to be symptomatic of the affective convolutions of this troubled summer. And it is in part through the metaphor of entanglement that I have approached this afterword. 'Entanglement' is in the title of this book, and it recurs in the book's contents as a refrain. If you tug on that particular conceptual thread, you will find that all sorts of practices, ideas and associations are woven into and around it. As a trope, 'entanglement' has been deployed in a wide range of theoretical and practical domains, including quantum mechanics, mathematics, digital technologies (the quantum internet), geometry (the orientation of an object), even the early twentieth-century military 'science' of wire obstacles. Most pertinently for me in this context, it is used widely in microbiology (e.g. mycorrhizal networks of fungi), Anthropocene ecologies, affect theory (a body's capacity to affect and be affected) and music. The word suggests something of the intricate complexities of embodiment, inter-subjectivity, connectivity and reciprocity; the passage of forces, intensities, atmospheres and information and the teeming traffic of what is at play in relational circuits and flows of all kinds. Entanglement asks questions of identities, boundaries, the singular and authorship, and proposes inseparability and mutuality of influence in a porous more-than-one. As dreams do, it insists on the inevitability of *nouement*, a knotting or knitting rather than the orderly schematic unraveling of a *dénouement*.

The collaborative devising of a duet performance necessarily entails diverse entanglements, as do all acts of interface and encounter in the life world: meeting another, or caring for another; or the quality of open attention to processes, emergent energies and rhythms other-than-one's-own that are required in such practices as, say, gardening, making music or riding a motorbike; just as they are in watching a live performance, in writing or reading …

Avenues of electricity (ghost dance)

Jill Orr lying face up on the beach in Melbourne in her mother's wedding dress, feeding the gulls with the loaves of bread and fish she has placed on her body and face. The Tibetan funeral practice of 'sky burial', in which a corpse is exposed on a mountain for consumption by carrion birds: excarnation, dispersal, transmigration, ascension. Francis Alÿs pushing a large block of ice through the streets of Mexico City until it melts away completely. A dark-suited man repeatedly scatters wooden chairs to create a clear path for a bare-footed somnambulist, a drifting woman with her eyes closed and arms outstretched, in Pina Bausch's *Café Müller*. The improvized encounter events of Bartabas and the majestic black stallion Zingaro, a horse never 'backed', in the suburbs of Paris. Steve Paxton's 'small dance', the first duet: micro-adjustments of balance in relation to gravity in the act of standing still. Steve Paxton sprinting through the studio at Dartington with an ecstatic, beaming blind man. Two blindfolded cowboys, Gregg Whelan and Gary Winters, repeating a simple line-dance sequence in silence for twelve hours, keeping time together by listening to each other's footsteps; as exhaustion starts to set in, others quietly join them in a collective 'ghost dance'. Aged five, pursued by a hostile swarm of bees whose hive I had disturbed while climbing a hollow tree in Zambia: the stings around my mouth … Playing frisbee with Stella the dog. Dog meetings. Dog walkings.

Things that happen

Ordinary affects are the varied, surging capacities to affect and to be affected that give everyday life the quality of a continual motion of relations, scenes, contingencies, and emergences. They're things that happen. They happen in impulses, sensations, expectations, daydreams, encounters, and habits of relating, in strategies and their failures, in forms of persuasion, contagion, and compulsion, in modes of attention, attachment, and agency, and in publics and social worlds of all kinds that catch people up in something that feels like something. (Stewart 2007: 1–2)

Entangled (spooky action)

Our microbial relationships are about as intimate as any can be. Learning more about these associations changes our experience of our own bodies and the places we inhabit. 'We' are ecosystems that span boundaries and transgress categories. Our selves emerge from a complex tangle of relationships only now becoming known. (Sheldrake 2020: 17–18)

Physics tells us that edges or boundaries are not determinate either ontologically or visually. When we come to the 'interface' between a coffee mug and a hand, it is not that there are x number of atoms that belong to a hand and y number of atoms that belong to the coffee mug [...] There are actually no sharp edges either: it is a well-recognised fact of physical optics that if one looks closely at an 'edge', what one sees is not a sharp boundary between light and dark but rather a series of light and dark bands – that is, a diffraction pattern. (Barad 2007: 156)

Einstein's derisive nickname for entanglement was what he called 'spooky action at a distance', but I was totally invested in the possibility of spooky action at a distance because for me that's a very interesting and accurate way to describe some of what occurs within the context of a jazz ensemble. (Fred Moten cited in Battaglia 2018)

How does a gathering become a 'happening', that is, greater than the sum of its parts? One answer is contamination. We are contaminated by our encounters; they change who we are as we make way for others. As contamination changes world-making projects, mutual worlds – and new directions – may emerge. Everyone carries a history of contamination; purity is not an option. One value of keeping precarity in mind is that it makes us remember that changing with circumstances is the stuff of survival. (Tsing 2015: 28)

A system of vital souls

A garden is perhaps the only human art that can be made for the pleasure of the other animals. Neither my poetry nor my prose has ever satisfied a finch or monarch, yet even the messiest patches of echinacea do. [...] A garden is a system of vital souls, every creature in it pushing and pulling, growing and receding, taking and contributing, beginning and ending, and myself, in that system, is both important and not, doing all the same things, respirating as the cats and the cardinals and soil microbes do. Even at its peak reckless chaos, or perhaps even most at its peak reckless chaos, the garden instructs through a series of multi-sensory inputs all of the living souls inside of it and in its way, harmonizes them, whispering into our

glandular aspects instructions soon transmitted to our cells. The potatoes and barberry and
the slugs and the gardener bask in the same, all-coordinating light. (Boyer 2019)

Care (push-pull)

When I last saw Gus, my neighbour in Western Australia, he was in his early 80s. A
delightful, sensitive man who had once been an engineer. We used to chat at length
over the fence or out walking with our two dogs. For over 40 years, Gus had been
caring for his bed-bound partner Anna; she had a rare brittle-bone condition so
extreme it meant that even a sneeze could result in a broken rib. Sometimes, we had
tea with Anna around her bed; she was both fragile and extraordinarily radiant. Out
with the dogs, over time, Gus revealed his frustration and exhaustion. After so many
years, the imperative to care for Anna, the push–pull of having to meet her every need
and demand, had ground him down. He loved Anna but wanted her to let go now, to
slip away; it was time, he said, while there was still time. Sometimes, despite himself,
the weight of his tiredness manifested as irritation or even anger towards Anna, and
he felt crippling guilt for not always being up to giving away his life for another. Gus
had an escape, and perhaps, he said, it was now 'the love of his life'. Once a week for
a few hours, he would go gliding by himself, and whenever he talked about it, he was
utterly transformed, lit up. The sheer joy of riding invisible thermals, the miracle of
soaring and hovering, the wedge-tailed eagles. The silence, adrift in skyspace with
the world laid out far below like 'a beautiful old faded carpet' (his words). Freed, for a
moment, from gravity and care, while Anna lay immobilized by her illness on her bed,
as light as a bird. When he came home afterwards, he said, he was troubled about
whether it was okay to feel such pleasure. I told him I felt sure it was, more than okay.
He invited me to come gliding with him. But then Anna died, and for months, Gus
was bereft. Grounded.

I am here

In the Mojave Desert, on the border of Nevada and California stands a phone booth. The
glass is shattered and the frame has six bullet holes. Each day, there are over one hundred
phone calls from every single continent, most often wrong numbers. Over the past few
years, the aluminum phone booth, which is owned by Pacific Bell, has become the great
switchboard of the world. It is the focalisation point of the multiple solitude of the invisible
community inhabiting the limbs of virtual space. Sometimes, as if by miracle, someone
answers: 'I am here', and the unknown caller replies: 'I'm glad you're there, that you
answered'. (Virilio 2000: 111)

World-building

1. *The astonishing reality of things and persons – this is the object of pure attention.*
2. *True attention does the work of* bringing forth. *It is the aperture through which the latency of things and persons become present. 'Mere' attention, ordinary attentiveness, is* useful, *standing in relation to the world like the opening, closing, entering, and exiting of the sensible doors in a well-maintained house. But unmixed attention – pure attention to* what cannot be used, to what no one already wants, to what promises no knowledge or gain – *does not require doors, because it* walks through walls.
3. *This true attention, given to objects, unerringly reveals the presence of others. [...]*
12. *This work is the work of freedom and understanding. It is a work, through attention, of world-building. This work is fundamentally political.* (Friends of Attention 2019)

Get out of the way

Throughout my collaboration with the performance maker Jane Mason over the past fifteen years or so, we have invariably returned to objects and their materiality as a foundational 'duet' in generating material. In the early days of devising a new performance, the studio is cluttered with all sorts of things. A box of rope and string. An odd collection of old spectacles. A pair of cowboy boots. A bucket of sand. Some silver body heat insulation sheets. An electric fan. Initially, our attention focuses on their saturated metaphoricity and on listening to the proliferative associations each of them may contain. What might they enable us to do? And what is made possible through the ways in which they constrain or compromise? Ultimately, however, it becomes a question of how to get out of their way sufficiently and create the conditions for at least some of these objects to happen in their vibrant and unpredictable particularity. How to awaken them, release their agencies and enable them to take (a) place? What do they want? What forms might their 'dance' or 'song' take? What kinds of 'weather' do they produce? Sometimes, I wonder whether the ideal, as yet only realized in fleeting wide-eyed moments, might in fact be to remove ourselves entirely and leave them free to play among themselves ...

Who me

Who's pimping who [...] ? (Prince 2004)

The other in all his or her forms gives me I. It is on the occasion of the other that I catch sight of me; or that I catch me at: reacting, choosing, refusing, accepting. It is the other who makes my portrait. Always. And luckily. (Cixous and Calle-Gruber 1997: 13)

Lila also said that the sensation she called dissolving margins [...] wasn't completely new to her. For example, she often had the sensation of moving for a few fractions of a second into a person or a thing or a number or a syllable, violating its edges. And the day her father threw her out the window she had felt absolutely certain, as she was flying toward the asphalt, that small, very friendly reddish animals were dissolving the composition of the street, transforming it into a smooth, soft material. (Ferrante 2012: 90–91)

Deep listening

Relations to and models of musicality have been central to my own experiences of making duets or working with duets over the years. It is much more than the dumb-but-true story I have told myself about why I might ever have started to make performances – that I really just wanted to be in a band and make music with others, that old dream of 'a falling together of accomplices' into 'a wondrous night web' (Ondaatje 1988: 151). The friendship at the heart of each of those duet relationships has been marked and consistently fed by an ongoing exchange of musical enthusiasms. And duet-making processes invite heightened attention to musical possibilities and difficulties, actualizing questions of accompaniment, harmony, counterpoint, call-and-response, dynamics, timbre and tonality, feel, rhythm, refrain, dissonance, the give and bend in a melodic line, the improvized solo, active silence, deep listening ...

Leaning

[Gillian] Welch and [David] Rawlings's music is deceptively complex, despite its simple components: two voices, two guitars, and four hands. [...] When Welch and Rawlings sing together, their voices fit so tightly that they seem welded. One of their newer songs—it doesn't yet have a title—is almost hypnotically slow and includes several passages sung in unison. Welch says that sometimes she loses the sense of which voice is hers and which belongs to Rawlings. Rawlings's ear for harmonic possibilities is impish. He does not always match Welch's phrasing. His line sometimes anticipates what Welch is singing, then meets hers and continues in another direction. He likes intervals that are closer than those commonly used. At certain moments of tension, their voices seem to be leaning against each other, like cards in a card house. (Wilkinson 2004)

Everything's a question of how you lean. If anything on wheels wants to corner or change direction, a centrifugal force comes into play. This force tries to pull us out of the bend into the straight, according to a law called the Law of Inertia, which always wants energy to save itself. In a corner situation it's the straight that demands least energy and so our fight starts. *By tipping our weight over into the bend, we shift the bike's centre of gravity and this counteracts the centrifugal force and the Law of Inertia! Birds do the same thing in the air.* (Berger 1995: 55–56)

An infinitely complex tune

All surfers are oceanographers, and in the area of breaking waves all are involved in advanced research. Surfers don't need to be told that when a wave breaks actual water particles, rather than simply the waveform, begin to move forward. They are busy working out more arcane relationships, like the one between tide and consistency, or swell direction and nearshore bathymetry. The science of surfers is not pure, obviously, but heavily applied. The goal is to understand, for the purpose of riding them, what the waves are doing, and especially what they are likely to do next. But waves dance to an infinitely complex tune. To a surfer sitting in the lineup trying to decipher the structure of a swell, the problem can indeed present itself musically. Are those waves approaching in 13/8 time, perhaps with seven sets an hour, and the third wave of every set swinging wide in a sort of dissonant crescendo? Or is this swell one of God's jazz solos, whose structure is beyond our understanding? (Finnegan 2015: 374)

Feel the song (a solo of duets)

During my encounters with the materials in this book, I have been revisited by a particular performance experience from the past, certainly one of the most memorable of my life. Curiously, this revenant event was a solo, although one woven exclusively from a diversity of duets of a particular kind. In our seismic moment – politically, socially, culturally, psychically – perhaps this performance's resilience as a memory comes from a feeling that it still seems to hold out (the glimmer of) a promise of a nuanced pedagogy of cooperative listening in relation to radical difference and hyphenated identities-in-motion.

In the mid-1990s, in Melbourne, I saw Anna Deavere Smith's *Fires in the Mirror: Crown Heights, Brooklyn and Other Identities*, an intimately epic solo performance about violent conflict between African Americans and Lubavitch Jews in Crown Heights, Brooklyn, in August 1991. Smith performed almost 30 different personae, all of them people implicated in the Crown Heights events in some way, using verbatim transcriptions of their words as recorded by her in interviews. As each new voice in this multi-perspectival oral history of fractious cultural relations was introduced, the name of the individual being performed was projected onto a screen behind Smith, like a caption or credit. Through voice and body, she stood in for African Americans, Jews, men and women, young and old, including the writer Ntozake Shange, the Reverend Al Sharpton and the distraught father of 7-year-old Gavin Cato, the Black child accidentally killed by a vehicle in a Lubavitcher motorcade. In these duets of empathic incorporation and witnessing, Smith allowed them to speak *through* her, her body hosted and re-pronounced their words. In the layered palimpsest complexity of these re-presentations, however, she was never quite transformed to the point of her own 'disappearance'.

Smith, the articulate shape-shifter, played with mimesis, sliding from persona to persona, sometimes temporarily retaining some residual attribute from the previous persona and thus producing a slippage or blur. Physically she did not impersonate as such; she signaled attributes in a mode related to the metonymic shorthands of Brechtian *gestus*. At the same time, she reproduced the precise vocal rhythms, cadences, inflections, tonalities, silences and other particularities of each individual's vocal *habitus* and speech gestures. In interviews, Smith has talked about the attempt in each of these 'duets' to 'feel the song' within a voice, and employing that song as a mnemonic register of a body and a way of performing self. The continuing presence throughout of her African American woman's body, her own voice and empathetic persona dipped in and out of focus to link and inform each of these polyphonic others who flared into ephemeral appearance then passed through.

Smith animated and inhabited the gap *between* them and thereby opened up an inter-subjective space beyond mimicry, a relational field of multiple subject positions co-existing. She acted as a cross-roads, agora or *bridge* (her own term) for these contradictory identities and testimonies, as if they were in dialogue with each other through her inter-locutory body; in this way, the apparently irreconcilable came into relation through her as materially unifying presence. They ghosted her and she ghosted them in this inhabiting of the dynamic axis between difference and identification, and the performance itself became a site for the negotiating and *working* of difference: in Smith's terms, 'a kind of cooperative dance' of 'identity in motion' (Smith 1993: xxv, xxxiii). Individuals had their say without their multiple perspectives being resolved into any singular point of view, and in the process, identity became plural and mutable, oppositional positions loosened to become less absolute, the border lands more fluid, the relations associational and on the move.

The main thing is that we both get out of the way. What can block the interview is 'us', your thinking about what you have to get done here, and my thinking about my own thoughts, opinions, biography, myself. The 'you' and the 'me' can prevent the 'inter'. It's not our views that matter, it's the inter. (James Hillman with Laura Pozzo 1983: 8)

My encounter with Félix Guattari changed a lot of things [...] We were only two but what was important for us was less our working together than this strange fact of working between the two of us. We stopped being 'author'. And these 'between-the-twos' referred back to other people, who were different on one side from on the other. The desert expanded, but in so doing became more populous [...] I stole Félix, and I hope he did the same for me. (Gilles Deleuze cited in Deleuze and Parnet 1987: 16–17)

Collaboration (the egret and the mule)

We write to what's becoming palpable in sidelong looks or a consistency of rhythm or tone. Not to drag things back to the land of the little judges, but to push the slo-mo button, to wait for what's starting up, to listen up for what's wearing out. We're tripwired by a tendency dilating. We make a pass at a swell in realism, and look for the hook. We back up at the hint of something. We butt in. We try to describe the smell; we trim the fat to pinpoint what seems to be the matter here [...] A thought hits at an angle. Subjects are surprised by their own acts. But everyone knows a composition when they see one. A scene can become a thing after only a few repetitions [...] Collaboration is a meeting of minds that don't match. (Berlant and Stewart 2019: 4–5)

Kathleen [Brennan] will start kind of talking in tongues, and I take it all down. She goes places [...] I can't get to those places. Too, I don't know [...] pragmatic. She's the egret of the family. I'm the mule. I write mostly from the world, the news, and what I really see from the counter, or hear. She's more impressionistic. She dreams like Hieronymus Bosch. She's been a lot of things. She drove a truck for a while. Had her own pilot's license. Worked as a soda jerk. Ran a big hotel in Miami. She was going to be a nun. When I met her, she was at the corner of nun or ruin. So together it's you wash, I'll dry. It works. (Tom Waits cited in Montandon 2006: 241–42)

The task is to become coherent enough in an incoherent world to engage in a joint dance of being that breeds respect and response in the flesh, in the run, on the course. And then to remember how to live like that at every scale, with all the partners. (Haraway 2003: 62)

References

Barad, Karen (2007), *Meeting the Universe Halfway: Quantum Physics and the Entanglement of Matter and Meaning*, Durham: Duke University Press.

Battaglia, Andy (2018), 'Every and All: Fred Moten's Oneness as a Poet, Theorist, and Artistic Muse', *ArtNews*, 27 March, https://www.artnews.com/art-news/artists/icons-fred-moten-9976/. Accessed 16 June 2020.

Berger, John (1995), *To the Wedding*, New York: Vintage.

Berlant, Lauren and Stewart, Kathleen (2019), *The Hundreds*, Durham: Duke University Press.

Boyer, Anne (2019), 'the same, all-coordinating light', *Mirabilary*, 20 December, https://mirabilary.substack.com/p/the-same-all-coordinating-light. Accessed 19 June 2020.

Cixous, Hélène and Calle-Gruber, Mireille (1997), *Rootprints: Memory and Life Writing*, London and New York: Routledge.

Deleuze, Gilles and Parnet, Claire (1987), *Dialogues*, New York: Columbia University Press.

Ferrante, Elena (2012), *My Brilliant Friend*, New York: Europa Editions.

Finnegan, William (2015), *Barbarian Days: A Surfing Life*, New York: Corsair/Penguin Random House.

Friends of Attention (2019), 'Twelve Theses on Attention', http://www.friendsofattention.net/documents/12theses. Accessed 21 June 2020.

Haraway, Donna (2000), *How Like a Leaf: An Interview With Thyrza Nichols Goodeve*, London and New York: Routledge.

Haraway, Donna (2003), *The Companion Species Manifesto: Dogs, People, and Significant Otherness*, Chicago: Prickly Paradigm Press.

Hillman, James, with Laura Pozzo (1983), *Inter Views*, Woodstock, CT: Spring Publications.

Montandon, Mac (ed.) (2006), *Innocent When You Dream: Tom Waits, The Collected Interviews*, London: Orion.

Ondaatje, Michael (1988), *In the Skin of a Lion*, London: Picador.

Prince (2004), 'Illusion, Coma, Pimp and Circumstance', *Musicology*, CD, Chanhassen: NPG Records.

Sheldrake, Merlin (2020), *Entangled Life: How Fungi Make Our Worlds, Change Our Minds and Shape Our Futures*, New York: Random House.

Smith, Anna Deavere (1993), *Fires in the Mirror*, New York: Anchor Books.

Stewart, Kathleen (2007), *Ordinary Affects*, Durham: Duke University Press.

Tsing, Anna Lowenhaupt (2015), *The Mushroom at the End of the World: On the Possibility of Life in Capitalist Ruins*, Princeton and Oxford: Princeton University Press.

Virilio, Paul (2000), 'The Twilight of the Grounds', in H. Chandès (ed.), *The Desert*, Paris and London: Fondation Cartier and Thames & Hudson, pp. 102–18.

Wilkinson, Alec (2004), 'The Ghostly Ones: How Gillian Welch and David Rawlings rediscovered country music', *The New Yorker*, 13 September, https://www.newyorker.com/magazine/2004/09/20/the-ghostly-ones. Accessed 14 June 2020.

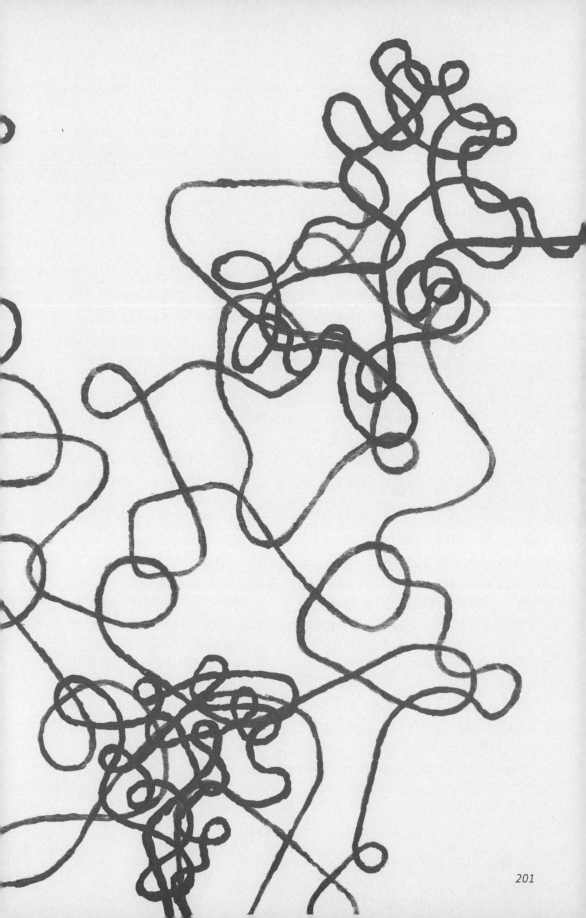

Contributors' Biographies

David Berman works in the Center for Research in String Theory at Queen Mary, University of London. His work is at the forefront of understanding the nature of space and time with a focus on moving beyond general relativity and generalizing the idea of geometry for spacetime. At Queen Mary, he developed a long-term cultural engagement programme and has collaborated with a variety of different artists over the last ten years. Before coming to London, he was previously employed as a research fellow at the Universities of Cambridge, Jerusalem, Groningen and Utrecht. https://www.qmul.ac.uk/spa/people/academics/profiles/dsberman.html

Teresa Brayshaw is a principal lecturer at Leeds School of Arts, a theatre practitioner, a writer, a teacher, a researcher and a qualified Feldenkrais practitioner. She was co-editor of the Training Grounds in the *International Journal of Theatre Dance and Performance Training* (2010–14) and has co-edited two of Routledge's best-selling Performance Readers: *The 21st Century Performance Reader* (Routledge, 2019) and *The 20th Century Performance Reader* (Third Edition, Routledge, 2013).

Season Butler is a writer, artist, dramaturg and lecturer in performance studies and creative writing. Her writing, research and art practice centre around intersectionality and narratives of otherness, isolation and negotiations with hope. Her debut novel, *Cygnet*, was published in spring 2019 and won the Writer's Guild 2020 Award for Best First Novel. www.seasonbutler.com

J. R. Carpenter is an artist, writer and researcher working across performance, print and digital media. Her web-based work *The Gathering Cloud* won the New Media Writing Prize 2016. Her print poetry collection *An Ocean of Static* was highly commended by the Forward Prizes 2018. Her collection *This is a Picture of Wind* was listed in *The Guardian*'s Best Poetry Books of 2020. She is Writer in Residence at University of Alberta, 2020–21. http://luckysoap.com

Karen Christopher is a collaborative performance maker, performer and teacher. Her UK-based company, Haranczak/Navarre Performance Projects, has been engaged in creating a series of duet performances over the past decade. Before relocating to Britain, Karen was a member of Chicago-based Goat Island performance group for 20 years until the group disbanded in 2009. Her writing on performance has appeared in TDR; Frakcija; Theatre, Dance and Performance Training and Green Letters, and in *Small Acts of Repair: Performance, Ecology and Goat Island* (Routledge, 2007), *Imagined Theatres* (Routledge, 2017), *The Creative Critic* (Routledge, 2018), *DIY* and *DIY too* (University of Chichester, 2014 and 2015) and *The Routledge Companion to Performance Philosophy* (Routledge, 2020). https://www.karenchristopher.co.uk

Sophie Grodin is a collaborative performance maker. Her practice is built around long-standing collaborations where the close relationship between a small group of people becomes part of the material used in the work. The tension between the individual and the group, the fine line between performing and not performing, and the collaboration developed with the audience over the course of a performance are all elements explored in this work. https://www.sophiegrodin.com

Eirini Kartsaki is a writer, performance maker and lecturer in East15 Acting School, University of Essex. She is the author of *Repetition in Performance: Returns and Invisible Forces* (Palgrave, 2017) and the editor of *On Repetition: Performance, Writing and Art* (Intellect, 2016). http://www.eirinikartsaki.com/research.php

Joe Kelleher is a writer and lecturer whose recent work has been concerned with questions of repetition and attention. He has been teaching at University of Roehampton since 1993 and a professor of theatre and performance since 2007. https:/pure.roehampton.ac.uk/portal/en/persons/joe-kelleher

Orit Kent is the co-founder and co-director of the Pedagogy of Partnership (PoP), an innovative research-based approach that re-envisions learning and cultivates the habits of wonder, empathy and responsibility and promotes connectivity. A long-time educator, teacher-educator, researcher and writer, Orit has written widely about peer- and relationship-based learning and is the co-author of the award-winning book *A Philosophy of Havruta*. She has been involved in the design and implementation of numerous professional and leadership development programs and was a lecturer in the education program at Brandeis University for many years. As a senior research associate at the Jack, Joseph and Morton Mandel Center for Studies in Jewish Education, Orit led a multi-year research and design effort focused on developing conceptual and practical tools for improving peer-based learning with elementary, middle school and university students. An alumna of the Wexner Graduate Fellowship, Orit holds a doctorate in Education and Jewish Studies from Brandeis University, an Ed.M. in Teaching and Learning from the Harvard Graduate School of Education and a BA in history from Yale University.

Andrea Milde (PhD, University of Sheffield, 2006), former senior lecturer at Nottingham Trent University, is a drama linguist, a video-ethnographer and works at Linguistics in Drama. Her research lies at the interface of spoken communication and the performing arts, with an interest in collaborative artistic text-production processes, rehearsal and studio working processes, creative collaboration, creativity and artistic practice. www.linguistics-in-drama.com

Mary Paterson is a writer who works across text, visual art and performance, and preferably in collaboration with other people. Alongside Maddy Costa and Diana Damian Martin, she runs *Something Other* and *The Department of Feminist Conversations*, two inter-related projects that bring together politics, performance and critical thinking. Recent publications include *Imagination and Potential* (Live Art Development Agency, 2016), *Joshua Sofaer: Performance | Objects | Participation* (co-edited with Roberta Mock; Intellect Books and the Live Art Development Agency, 2020) and *Challenging Archives* (co-authored with Maddy Costa; University of Bristol, 2020).

Rajni Shah is an artist whose practice is focused on listening and gathering as creative and political acts. Key projects – always created alongside and in collaboration with others – include *hold each as we fall* (1999), *The Awkward Position* (2003–04), *Mr Quiver* (2005–08), *small gifts* (2006–08), *Dinner with America* (2007–09), *Glorious* (2010–12), *Experiments in Listening* (2014–15), *Lying Fallow* (2014–15), *Song* (2016), *I don't know how (to decolonize myself)* (2018), *Feminist Killjoys Reading Group* (2016–20) and *Listening Tables* (2019–20). In 2021, Rajni's first monograph, *Experiments in Listening*, will be published as part of the Performance Philosophy Series with Rowman & Littlefield.

Litó Walkey is an artist of Canadian and Greek origins based in Berlin. Moving between writing, choreography and performance, her work engages strategies of collaboration, proliferation and translation to activate critical ecologies of attention. Recent projects were developed with Weld Company and Fylkingen (Stockholm); BCN and MEZANNINE (Porto); Tanzfabrik and Hebbel am Ufer (Berlin). Following her nine-year teaching position at HZT Inter-University Center for Dance Berlin, Litó initiated a publication on the entanglement of artistic and pedagogic practices. From 2002 to 2009, she performed and taught internationally with the Chicago-based performance group Goat Island. She teaches at the Arts Universities of Stockholm, Helsinki and Copenhagen and advises choreographic work.

David Williams has made, taught and written about contemporary performance in the United Kingdom, Europe and Australia since the 1980s. As well as teaching for many years at Dartington College of Arts and Royal Holloway University of London, as a dramaturg, he has collaborated with practitioners including Lone Twin, Jane Mason and Action Hero. Recent projects include the duet *Night Flying*, devised and performed with Jane Mason.

Jemima Yong is a performance maker and photographer. She is Sarawakian, born in Singapore, and has developed her artistic practice in London, UK, where she is currently based. Collaboration and experimentation are central to her work. Recent performances include *Something in Your Voice* with Emergency Chorus and *Marathon* with JAMS, which received the Oxford Samuel Beckett Theatre Trust Award 2018 and was presented by the Barbican Centre. Jemima's photography has been featured by the BBC, Time Out, *The Guardian*, *Swazi Observer* and *The Straits Times*. She is an associate artist at Forest Fringe and is one fifth of DARC (Documentation Action Research Collective). Jemima is an alumni of United World Colleges, Royal Central School of Speech and Drama and The Curious School of Puppetry.

Acknowledgements

This book began as a twinkle in the eye of CJ Mitchell, who imagined it before any of us who contributed directly to its contents did. After dreaming it into existence, he worked tirelessly in the background providing the kind of administration that is essential in making a book happen. He knows how to follow up and is meticulous with the detail work. As Karen, I want to thank my co-editor Mary for working alongside me to come up with a scheme for how to contextualize my sense of the duet form and its affordances, and for always fathoming the seemingly unfathomable and doing so with equal parts calm, cool, artistic integrity and activist fervour.

Our thanks to each of the contributors who gave us their time and individual flair embedded in the words and images they have strung together for this collection, including David Caines, the book designer, who painted some enigmatic entangled lines for us.

We are grateful to Jelena Stanovnik, Tim Mitchell, Sophia Munyengeterwa and the staff of Intellect who smiled and said this will be a good book.

Duet partners in Haranczak/Navarre's duet series are due continued thanks for their devotion to the struggle of getting along with a fellow human to face the work of spinning performance works out of thin air. They are Gerard Bell, Teresa Brayshaw, Sophie Grodin, Rajni Shah and Tara Fatehi Irani. Thanks also for support received for the duet series from Chelsea Theatre (under the direction of Francis Alexander) in the incipient stages and from Chisenhale Dance Space (under the direction of Justin Hunt) during TwoFold, our retrospective festival of duets. And many thanks to the venues who showed any of the duets in the series.

Karen wishes to thank Aoife Monks and Daniel Oliver of Queen Mary, University of London, for writing retreats organized for their artist research fellows during the early days of the COVID-19 pandemic making it possible to think clearly for the last bits of pulling this collection together.

Mary would like to thank Karen for all her kindness, conversation and companionship and also for the packages of wool and tree bark that made it possible to get through the first pandemic lockdown. And Mary would like to thank Ross and Arlo Miller, for everything.

Finally, Karen wishes to thank the author and artist Shelley Jackson, a duet partner from a place long ago and who made me a word in her story.

First published in the UK in 2021 by Intellect,
The Mill, Parnall Road, Fishponds, Bristol, BS16 3JG, UK

First published in the USA in 2021 by Intellect,
The University of Chicago Press, 1427 E. 60th Street, Chicago, IL 60637, USA

A catalogue record for this book is available from the British Library.

Book design: David Caines
www.davidcaines.co.uk

Copy editor: MPS

Production editor: Sophia Munyengeterwa

Print ISBN 978-1-78938-504-5
ePDF ISBN 978-1-78938-505-2
ePUB ISBN 978-1-78938-506-9

Printed and bound by Gomer

To find out about all our publications, please visit our website.
There you can subscribe to our e-newsletter, browse or download
our current catalogue and buy any titles that are in print.

www.intellectbooks.com.

This is a peer-reviewed publication.